Women in Ministry

Women in Ministry

Paul's Advice to Timothy in Its Historical Setting

Edgar Stubbersfield

WIPF & STOCK · Eugene, Oregon

WOMEN IN MINISTRY
Paul's Advice to Timothy in Its Historical Setting

Copyright © 2022 Rachel Stubbersfield. All rights reserved. Except for brief quotations in critical publications or reviews, no part of this book may be reproduced in any manner without prior written permission from the publisher. Write: Permissions, Wipf and Stock Publishers, 199 W. 8th Ave., Suite 3, Eugene, OR 97401.

Wipf & Stock
An Imprint of Wipf and Stock Publishers
199 W. 8th Ave., Suite 3
Eugene, OR 97401

www.wipfandstock.com

PAPERBACK ISBN: 978-1-6667-3433-1
HARDCOVER ISBN: 978-1-6667-9007-8
EBOOK ISBN: 978-1-6667-9008-5

05/23/22

Scripture quotations taken from the (NASB®) New American Standard Bible®, Copyright © 1960, 1971, 1977, 1995, 2020 by The Lockman Foundation. Used by permission. All rights reserved.www.lockman.org

Contents

Acknowledgments | vii
Introduction | ix

1. Cultural and Religious Expectation | 1
2. The Ephesian Heresy and Ministry Roles | 26
3. Exposition of First Timothy 2:8–15 | 60
4. Bringing the Threads Together | 83

Conclusion | 99
Bibliography | 103

Acknowledgments

I AM GRATEFUL TO the Rev. Dr. Alan Gordon who encouraged me to start studying again. I appreciated his grace and perseverance and trust that through his encouragement I have written something that is useful to at least half of Christ's church.

Introduction

As a young boy growing up, I attended the local Congregational church where my parents were members. There is nothing like a Congregational minister in a Geneva gown to lend gravitas to a service! The members were proud of a local girl made good. She had gone off and studied to be a minister and was the first ordained female Congregational minister in Queensland, Australia. Occasionally she would come home to preach. Unfortunately, her shrill voice cut a very discordant note to my poor childish brain! Geneva gown or not, nothing could restore the gravitas. On such trivia can matters of great importance be weighed.

When the angel, and then Jesus himself, instructed the two women to tell the disciples that Jesus had risen (Matt 28:7–10), did the men sit around debating the rights and wrongs of women being the first to proclaim the gospel of the risen Lord (1 Cor 15:1–4)? Did they debate about whether the message should have been delivered in a more masculine voice? Rather, in their bewilderment they raced each other to the tomb. On the mission fields, for centuries, many men and women still run to the saving words of Christ's empty tomb preached through women. Historically they

Introduction

have made up the larger part of the missionary numbers and this has been also where the greatest successes have been achieved. It is undeniable that God has blessed their ministry. But is this because he has chosen to because it is in accordance with his will or is it reluctantly out of necessity. Necessity because men would not heed the call!

In an age where we are very conscious of the evil of racism, are Christians guilty of blatant racism if we demand a more pure, female-free gospel for their western churches than is considered acceptable in the third world? My Congregational church in the 1950s and '60s could accept a female minister as it had become very liberal and, for many in that denomination, the Bible was reduced to merely a book of good suggestions. But for those who believe the Bible has ultimate authority, the issue of women in ministry remains a seriously debated topic in Australia, my homeland.

This subject must be approached cautiously as the historic view of a subordinate role for women is still the situation in the Roman Catholic and Eastern Orthodox churches, which makes up about 60 percent of believers, and probably 90 percent of Christians are not concerned about the fact that most pastors are men.[1] While lip service is given to the ordination of women in many evangelical and charismatic/pentecostal churches, actual practice can be very different. It must be questioned whether this is all largely a matter of navel gazing by a western church that no longer regards the Bible as the Word of God and authoritative. The changed role for women, in many cases, can simply be the accommodation of the declining western church to the same changes in an increasingly post-Christian society. The church's role should be to challenge culture with the utter seriousness of sin and the power of the crucified Christ to save, forgive, and transform. Far from making the church more appealing, "denominations that have ordained women have generally seen annual reductions in attendance year by year."[2] The western church has lost sight of

---

1. Yarbrough, "Familiar Paths," 228, 236.

2. Robert Yarbrough quotes data from the mainline American denominations, United Church of Christ, the Evangelical Lutheran Church, the

Introduction

how liberating even the traditional view portrayed in 1 Tim 2 is for many women, particularly those coming from regions where Sharia law is practiced. Conversely, the western church does not consider the peril such women would be placed in should they take an open leadership role.³ Forcing an egalitarian role for women in Christian ministry would hamper the advance of God's kingdom rather than advance it in many spheres. This discussion will be more a matter of what is permitted, not how things should be and are across all cultures and political settings.

Probably the most commonly cited reference to prohibit women in ministry is found in 1 Tim 2:11–12: "A woman must quietly receive instruction with entire submissiveness. 12 But I do not allow a woman to teach or to exercise authority over a man, but to remain quiet." Since the rise of feminism, in the 1960s and '70s, there have been many publications that have provided strong exegetical reasons to seriously suggest that long held non-inclusive interpretations may be incorrect. They promote their understanding that it is possible to hold true to the scriptures and the gospel and yet also embrace female ministry. This small book is part of that discussion and one that I trust strengthens the case for full acceptance of more than half of our membership.

Your book is made up of this introduction and four sections:

Introduction. As authorship of Pastoral Epistles is very contentious, my basis for accepting Pauline authorship needs to be briefly explained.

Presbyterian Church (USA), the Episcopal Church, and the United Methodist Church, which show a 3.4 percent reduction in membership from 2007–14 compared with 0.9 percent for evangelical protestant churches. Yarbrough, "Familiar Paths," 237.

3. There is a a very moving application of the traditional understanding of 1 Tim 2:8–15 by Yarbrough in the setting of Muslim background believers in a country where the government was genocidal and actively hostile to Christianity. It was a country where males were angry and violent, women were uneducated and suffered female genital mutilation, which made marriages difficult. There, leadership came with a massively increased risk of persecution, something that was particularly nasty for women. Yarbrough, "Familiar Paths," 262–74.

Introduction

Chapter 1. Observation of female participation in widely different practices outside of Christianity would have led to expectations about participation in or alternatively, exclusion from ministry roles. Drawing heavily from classical sources, the Mishna and Talmud, this chapter explains what that would have been.

Chapter 2. Timothy was sent to Ephesus to address false teachers that were troubling the church and affecting its reputation. The purpose of church officers and implications drawn from the requirements for and role of elders and deacons in First Timothy and Titus will be discussed. Paul considered it vital that the church be highly regarded by those outside the church and well-regarded role models were needed to lead the church. This all impacts upon Paul's instructions regarding women in ministry.

The direct and indirect evidence of what is known of women in Christian ministry outside of the Pastoral Epistles with special emphasis on Ephesus is also examined. Classical sources and Rom 16 will be referred to. Other matters arising from First and Second Timothy and Titus will be discussed (apart from 1 Tim 2:8–15).

Chapter 3. Here I provide an exposition of 1 Tim 2:8–15 where the apparent total ban on women in ministry and their subordinate role will be assessed. The range of alternative interpretations are examined.

Chapter 4. I will draw all the threads together and make a contemporary application of what is learned from the preceding chapters. A conclusion is drawn.

Authorship of the Pastoral Epistles

Most Christians have little, if any, interest in the arguments of scholars as to who wrote First and Second Timothy and Titus and will simply accept these books as God-breathed and useful for teaching. If that is you, I suggest that you skip the next few pages and go straight to chapter 1. But you may be intrigued, and perhaps even curious, to learn that many people (not all of them are men) assert that a major document used to exclude women from ministry is a forgery!

Introduction

Paul's injunction in 1 Tim 2:8–15 forms a large part of the case used to deny a ministry role for women, but did Paul actually write these words? The role of women's ministry in the Pastoral Epistles cannot be considered apart from this difficult matter of authorship. While the Pastoral Epistles claim to be written by Paul, this is far from universally accepted by academics now. Instead, it is claimed that non-Pauline authorship is the view held by 80–90 percent[4] of modern scholars with the date of authorship being about 80–100 AD.[5] Though the traditional view still has its supporters, for many years the opinion was that the letters, as they stand, were composed by some "Pauline enthusiast"[6] and derive from the sub-apostolic age, perhaps even as late as the middle of the second century. Non-Pauline authorship was said to be one of the "assured results of scholarship,"[7] so certain that when the New English Bible translates 1 Tim 1:2, it refers to Timothy as "his trueborn son." The claim has even been made that these "forgeries" were written to counteract women already in a ministry role as is seen with *The Acts of Paul and Thecla*[8] or countering the effects of the heretic Marcion (c. 85–160).

Critics of Pauline authorship refer to the writer as an imitator or a devout "Paulinist" and studiously avoid the word "forger" with its moral stigma as it is said to prejudice the issue.[9] Attempts are made to sanitize the motives of the writer by claiming that it would almost have been an injustice for the real author to use his name as he was writing what he believed would have been the thoughts of Paul.[10] It is a further, though unproven claim that the church was

---

4. Scholarship is changing opinion about pseudonymity as a "significant number of commentaries in English in the last twenty years hold to Pauline authorship." Mounce, *Pastoral Epistles*, xlviii.
5. Brown, *Introduction*, 668.
6. Kelly, *Commentary*, 4–5.
7. Mounce, *Pastoral Epistles*, lxxxiv.
8. Johnson, *First and Second*, 205.
9. Guthrie, *New Testament*, 645–46.
10. Guthrie, *New Testament*, 645.

Introduction

aware of their pseudonymous origin and that their true origin was only lost to later generations.[11]

The subject of authorship brings with it the uncomfortable question of authority. Exploring the implications for authority is reserved for chapter 4. This assessment of the role of women's ministry in the Pastoral Epistles assumes, on the basis of the strong defense in recent years by William Mounce[12] and Gordon Fee[13] and others, that they are indeed Pauline. A brief overview and critique of one writer's argument for pseudonymity[14] is helpful as I believe that the logical framework of their argument appears faulty.

One of the standard approaches to pseudonymity occurs in Martin Dibelius and Hans Conzelmann's *The Pastoral Epistles*.[15] They admit that there is no single overarching argument that demands that First and Second Timothy are not Pauline. By interpreting the whole in light of the problems they see, they do not exegete the text in its totality. Instead, much of what is significant and new in these books can be understood in the light of the evolution of the Pauline churches.[16]

Dibelius and Conzelmann recognized that Second Timothy "seems to be a genuine personal communication"[17] to Timothy and is full of Paul's personal idiosyncrasies.[18] However, despite Second Timothy's appearance as genuine,[19] it is claimed quite categorically

---

11. Guthrie, *New Testament*, 645.

12. Mounce, *Pastoral Epistles*, lxxxiii-cxxix.

13. Fee, *1 and 2 Timothy*, 23–31.

14. A much-expanded critique is found in my *Introduction to the Pastoral Epistles*.

15. Dibelius and Conzelmann, *Pastoral*, 1–10.

16. Dibelius and Conzelmann cite Hans Von Campenhausen *Ecclesiastical Authority and Spiritual Power* to justify the un-Pauline character of church order in the Pastorals. Dibelius and Conzelmann, *Pastoral*, 3; Von Campenhausen, *Ecclesiastical Authority*, 106–19. I accept the church order is different from that seen in Acts but that does not prove pseudonymity.

17. Dibelius and Conzelmann, *Pastoral*, 7.

18. Dibelius and Conzelmann, *Pastoral*, 7.

19. Far from being an obvious literary fraud, in all the Pastorals "there are many passages that give the impression of imitation." Dibelius and

Introduction

"to be sure, the Pastorals are pseudonymous."[20] Despite this, they can elicit no reason why a fraudulent work would be written.[21]

For Dibelius and Conzelmann, their conclusion depends on "the convergence of a whole series of arguments."[22] They believe that one of the strongest in this "series of arguments" is the language of the Pastorals. They reject the statistical approach to the language as inadequate[23] and concede that alternate theories, such as a fragmentary or secretary hypotheses,[24] can explain most of the new words.[25]

They argue that, because First Timothy is considered to be pseudonymous, and because First and Second Timothy had the same author, then Second Timothy must be pseudonymous also. It seems to be safer to argue that, because there is no convincing case against a Pauline authorship for Second Timothy, and because the argument against a Pauline authorship of First Timothy is particularly weak, then their admittedly mutual author would most likely be Paul.

The argument appears to hinge on one question. Was Paul released from the Roman imprisonment recorded in Acts which

---

Conzelmann, *Pastoral*, 4.

20. Dibelius and Conzelmann, *Pastoral*, 7.
21. Dibelius and Conzelmann, *Pastoral*, 2–3.
22. Dibelius and Conzelmann, *Pastoral*, 1.
23. Dibelius and Conzelmann, *Pastoral*, 2.

24. It is difficult to write when in heavy Roman chains so having Paul use Luke the Physician as his amanuensis would explain the alleged higher standard of koine Greek and also the fact that thirty-seven of the "new" Pauline words are found in Luke/Acts. A further thirty-seven words found in both the Pastoral Epistles and Luke/Acts only rarely occur in the New Testament. Mounce, *Pastoral Epistles*, cxxvii.

25. The claim is that most of the new words reflect Hellenistic not New Testament Greek. Dibelius and Conzelmann, *Pastoral*, 2–3. This is refuted by Donald Guthrie who claims virtually all the words that occur once (hapaxes) in the Pastoral Epistles are known in Greek literature by the middle of the first century and half are in the Septuagint, which Paul would have been intimately acquainted with. A considerable number of the "new" Pauline words are found in other books of the New Testament. Guthrie, *Pastoral*, 634–35.

Introduction

allowed him to evangelize the west?²⁶ There is not one early church tradition that says Paul died at the end of his first and only imprisonment without being released.²⁷

It must be noted that the following chapter dealing with the cultural setting of Ephesus could be irrelevant to many scholars who reject Pauline authorship. Dibelius and Conzelmann are typical when they say that "the situation of the origin of the Pastorals is not clarified at any point."²⁸

---

26. Dibelius and Conzelmann, *Pastoral*, 3.
27. Mounce, *Pastoral Epistles*, lvi.
28. Dibelius and Conzelmann, *Pastoral*, 5.

1

Cultural and Religious Expectation

Why We Need to Know the Background

THE NEW TESTAMENT IS a fairly obvious place to start to determine what a Christian viewpoint on women in ministry should be. For all that, it is hard to read it without starting from a twenty-first-century understanding of faith, life, and even the present acceptance of the equality of men and women. Quite unintentionally, this can cause the reader to force onto those words what they want to see instead of letting those same words inform their opinion. This chapter looks at the nature of the different religions practiced in Ephesus and a woman's role in them so the reader can grasp the environment, experience, and hopes that female Christian converts came from. It would have molded both female and male expectancy about ministry.

The books that are looked to for guidance were written to a vastly different world. Those living in the Greco-Roman world of the mid '60s of the first century would not recognize ours just as we have trouble comprehending theirs. It should leave us questioning how much of what we read in the New Testament was molded by the life situation the books were written into and how

Women in Ministry

much relates to matters that transcend time and place. If we say that culture in some ways is reflected in the instructions found in those books, does this then have an impact upon our understanding of a woman's role in the church when faced with a different and vastly changed culture?

Christianity, and the role of women in its ministry, did not develop in a vacuum. First and Second Timothy, the focus of this book, were written to Paul's emissary in the Greek city of Ephesus in Asia Minor. What was that first-century culture like for a woman in that culture? Plutarch, a contemporary Greek writer's advice to a bride and groom, does not paint a good picture for the status of female Gentiles in the New Testament period and gives us a good reference point to compare against our present situation:

> The women of Egypt, by inherited custom, were not allowed to wear shoes, so that they should stay at home all day; and most women, if you take from them gold-embroidered shoes, bracelets, anklets, purple, and pearls, stay indoors.
>
> Teano,[1] in putting her cloak about her, exposed her arm. Somebody exclaimed, "A lovely arm." "But not for the public," said she. Not only the arm of the virtuous woman, but her speech as well, ought to be not for the public, and she ought to be modest and guarded about saying anything in the hearing of outsiders, since it is an exposure of herself; for in her talk can be seen her feelings, character, and disposition.
>
> Pheidias made the Aphrodite of the Eleans[2] with one foot on a tortoise, to typify for womankind keeping at home and keeping silence. For a woman ought to do her talking either to her husband or through her husband, and she should not feel aggrieved if, like the flute-player, she makes a more impressive sound through a tongue not her own.[3]

---

1. Born in the sixth century BC, she is the first known female mathematician and was a student of Pythagoras.

2. Elis, an historic region in the western part of the Peloponnese peninsular of Greece.

3. Plutarch, *Conj. Praec.* 30–32.

Cultural and Religious Expectation

The importance of this chapter, which looks at the role of women in Ephesus, is that the city was the focus of much of the New Testament. Tradition says that many of its books were written to, from, near to, or sent to localities near this city. Any discussion on the subject of women in ministry based on two letters written to Ephesus must start with an understanding of the religious and cultural situation that existed at the time. Equally, an understanding of the situation in Ephesus will inform our understanding of much of the New Testament. Without this understanding, the transformation for women in our society wrought by the gospel coming to a pagan world, is hidden from us.

Ephesus and Artemis

When Paul stepped ashore at Ephesus c. 52–53 AD in what is now Turkey, it was a Greek city but under increasing influence from Rome. Though long established it was also a relatively "new" city as a severe earthquake in 23 AD had damaged many public buildings. These were rebuilt over time by public donations. With a population at that time thought to be about 100,000,[4] Ephesus was rapidly becoming "the greatest and first metropolis of Asia." However, it had not been smooth sailing for the city. Corinth, across the Aegean Sea from Ephesus, was destroyed by the Romans in 146 BC and rebuilt as a Roman colony in 44 BC. Ephesus did not escape the political and economic troubles of the first century BC, particularly when Mark Anthony plundered the Temple of Artemis. But the city was very different in the way it had been accommodating to conquerors. We perceive the iron rule of Rome from our perspective of accomplished history, but it may not have appeared too secure in the first century as there had been catastrophic civil wars and more would follow after the death of Nero. Until the rule of Vespasian (69–79) it may have been very uncertain where one should place allegiance.

---

4. Baugh, "Foreign World," 29.

Women in Ministry

It would be hard to find a modern comparison to the relationship between the city and its god. Many coins show an image of Artemis and her temple as these represented Ephesus itself. Our clear-cut distinction between religious and secular did not apply. A person belonged to the city and the city belonged to Artemis. Harmony in all relationships of life and with the gods came through the practice of *Eusebia*, described by Isocrates as:

> ... not [destroying] any institution of their fathers and to introduce nothing which was not approved by custom, believing that reverence consists, not in extravagant expenditures, but in disturbing none of the rites which their ancestors had handed on to them. And so also the gifts of the gods were visited upon them, not fitfully or capriciously, but seasonably both for the ploughing of the land and for the ingathering of its fruits.[5]

Despite foreign rule, or perhaps because of it, the city was striving as much as possible to retain and revive its Greek laws and customs in a Roman empire.[6] There is no reason to believe it was significantly less patriarchal than any other Greek city, despite retaining its strong allegiance to the goddess Artemis Ephesia.

Unlike our present secular western society, Ephesus had a religious environment that strongly pervaded all areas of life for both men and women. A woman converted to Christianity from either paganism or Judaism would have carried with her much of her expectation of her potential role in ministry from her understanding of what they might expect in the many religions that flourished in the city. Likewise, men who permitted some freedoms, and imposed restrictions on women, are likely to expect the same to continue, at least to some degree. However, Ephesus was a city where women could at least dream of freedom from male domination. There the worship of the goddess Artemis was centered around

---

5. Isocrates, *Arop.* 7.30. This was a long-lived belief. Isocrates lived 436–338 BC and the same belief in *eusebia* is found in Aelius Aristides (117–81 AD). Aelius Aristides, *Or.* 24.42.

6. Baugh, "Foreign World," 28.

Cultural and Religious Expectation

powerful and independent women who were far from the gullible or weak women that Paul mentioned (2 Tim 3:6–7).

Strabo, who visited Ephesus not many years before Paul, speaks about these women when he recorded both the mythological and the historical account of the founding of Ephesus.[7] The myth said that Smyrna, an Amazon,[8] took control of the city. After its capture, the Amazon leader Hippolyte set up the statue of Artemis and started an annual dance around the city with weapons and shields.[9] The Amazons would in turn be driven away by the Greek invasion c. 1068 BC.[10]

The worship of Ephesian Artemis was a practice described "as far more ancient than their [the Greeks] coming."[11] Most likely the Greeks assimilated a local earth goddess with their own Artemis as she was worshipped differently from elsewhere in the Greek world. Artemis became the most popular god in Anatolia,[12] held "in honor above all the gods."[13] Pausanias (second century AD) claims this arose because of the association with the Amazons. When explaining her prominence, he says that "three other points as well have contributed to her renown, the size of the temple, surpassing all buildings among men, the eminence of the city of the Ephesians and the renown of the goddess who dwells there."[14] The temple, known as the *Artemision*, was approximately four times the size of the Parthenon in Athens!

---

7. Strabo, *Geogr.* 14.1.5; Pausanias, *Descr.* 4.31.8.

8. These were a mythological race of fierce women warriors so committed to martial arts that they removed their right breasts (*amaza* = breastless) so it did not impede their javelin throwing. Strabo, *Geogr.* 11.5.3; Evans and Porter, *Dictionary*, 318.

9. Described in Callimachus, *Hymn.* 3.238 ff: Evans and Porter, *Dictionary*, 318.

10. Pausanias, *Descr.* 4:31.8, 7.2.6–9. Refer Cornelius Tacitus. *Ann.* 3.61.1 for their importance.

11. Pausanias, *Descr.* 7.2.6.

12. An area comprising most of modern Turkey.

13. Pausanias, *Descr.* 4.31.8.

14. Pausanias, *Descr.* 4.31.8.

Women in Ministry

The notion of powerful independent women was reinforced in the Artemis cult as, unlike other Greek goddesses, Artemis Ephesia, like the Amazons, had no need of a male partner. Images of the Amazons stood in Artemis' temple,[15] and their victories were remembered annually in the processions around the city's monuments. These processions remembered their myths and history reinforcing that Artemis, a female god, acted in history as protector and sustainer of the city and its people.[16] Myths, an important part of Artemis's worship, were "maps" which "expressed the life-power of Ephesus"[17] and explained the relationship of Ephesus to its gods and heroes. Some were secret and were related to a specific festival and time.[18] They could be used to initiate into the tribe, bring salvation and give meaning through continuity with the past.[19] The reciter called upon the creative and sustaining power of Artemis by remembering her myths.

The famous statement by Demosthenes (fourth century BC) about the roles of women in Greek culture has bearing on understanding the role of Artemis Ephesia—"Mistresses we keep for the sake of pleasure, concubines for the daily care of our persons, but wives to bear us legitimate children and to be faithful guardians of our households."[20] Greek Artemis is associated with virginity, but the later cult image of Ephesian Artemis shows her with many egg shaped breasts.[21] Western culture tends to eroticize all female roles but not so the Greek. The goddess was fully gendered but was not sexual. Hanging breasts, seen as grotesque in erotic art, were respected in a wife and mother. In her "nutrient breasts that overflow

---

15. Pliny the Elder, *Nat.* 34.19.53.
16. LiDonnici, "Image of Arteimis," 394.
17. Strelan, *Paul*, 57.
18. Strabo, *Geogr.* 14.1.20.
19. Strelan, *Paul*, 55.

20. Demosthenes, *In Neaeram.* 59.122. Herodotus is surprised and suspicious about the concept of a man being sexually obsessed with his wife. Herodotus, *Hist.* 1.8–12.

21. For a discussion of alternate interpretations of these protuberances see Thomas, *At Home in the City*, 86–87, and LiDonnici, "Image of Artemis," 392.

with sustaining milk"[22] she would be seen rather as the legitimate wife of the city and protectress of family, politics, and the universe's stability. This is why Artemis could be worshipped by virgins, celibate priestesses, and married women without any paradox.

The signs of the zodiac were also displayed around the neck of her cult image, and the *Ephesia Grammata* (Ephesian letters) were written indistinctly and obscurely around her feet, girdle, and crown. (These are discussed later in this chapter.) Other than through her image, the goddess could be seen in dreams[23] and epiphanies.[24] Strabo says that on her birthday, May 6,[25] mysteries were performed,[26] but little is known of their nature or significance. "Mysteries" were a common feature of many Ephesian religions, but what is known refers to their public rites, not to the secrets that satisfied their need for "a personal, spiritual, redemptive, and universal religion."[27] It is claimed that most Greek religions were universal in their acceptance of people irrespective of social status or sex.[28] While she was not primarily a goddess of magic, there was an association with the worship of Artemis and her mysteries with magic. The role of women in magic will be discussed further on in this section.

Her worship, which involved sacrifice and offering incense, is believed to be similar to that of other pagan deities. She was served by virgins and eunuchs (effectively male equivalents), though by Strabo's time the use of eunuchs had ceased.[29] Two hundred years later, Pausanias would say that Artemis was served by priests, called king bees, who would be chaste for twelve months, but were not eunuchs.[30] Reference has been found to a high priest and

---

22. LiDonnici, "Image of Artemis," 408.
23. Strabo, *Geogr.* 4.1.3–4; Achilles Tatius, *Leuc. Clit.* 4.1.4.
24. Strelan, *Paul*, 52.
25. Possibly on other occasions as well. Hawthorne and Martin, *Dictionary of Paul*, 250.
26. Strabo, *Geogr.* 14.1.20.
27. Gritz, *Paul*, 31–32.
28. Gritz, *Paul*, 32, 35.
29. Strabo, *Geogr.* 14.1.23.
30. Pausanias, *Descr.* 8:13:1.

priestess.³¹ The presence of priests was unusual for a Greek city as goddesses were normally served by priestesses and the gods were served by priests.³²

According to the myths, Leto, a titan, was impregnated by Zeus and conceived twins, the daughter was Artemis and the son, Apollo. Artemis was born fist and became the midwife for the delivery of her brother. This act saw her as being the god who protected in childbirth.³³ When Paul was in Ephesus, the girls were normally married in their early to mid-teens and very likely died in their mid-twenties and, if they lived, could be a grandmother in their thirties. Death during childbirth was so common that a successful delivery would be received with deep relief and viewed as an escape.³⁴ As an example of Artemis's help through childbirth, her temple was destroyed, it was claimed, by an arsonist in 356 BC³⁵ on the same night that Alexander the Great was born. The excuse given by Plutarch for Artemis not looking after her temple was that she was too preoccupied with Alexander's delivery to save her burning temple.³⁶

Artemis was presented as a personal savior and helper³⁷ who heard prayers. Despite her role in childbirth, she "is seen as a champion of chastity, not in a ritual context but in everyday behavior, that is, a supporter of chastity as a moral value, a conventional Greek attitude."³⁸ Her female devotees took pride in their modest piety.³⁹ Artemis is sometimes called *Lysizones*, the "releaser of the girdle." Girls put this on at puberty and removed it after their first

31. Baugh, "Cult Prostitution," 167.
32. Baugh, "Foreign World," 35.
33. Callimachus, *Hymn. Dian.* 20–25
34. Baugh, "Foreign World," 42, 53.
35. Strabo, *Geogr.* 14.1.22
36. Plut. *Alex.* 3.3–5
37. Strelan, *Paul*, 51. Pausanias makes numerous references to Artemis being called "savior" throughout the Greek world, e.g., 1.40.2; 1.44.4; 3.22.12; 3.23.10.
38. Thomas, "At Home," 96.
39. Brough, "Cult Prostitution," 163.

intercourse at which time it was dedicated to Artemis.[40] A goddess that protected women was valued.

This godess was also the protector of young men[41] and men worshipped her in private.[42] They probably lived ten years longer than women.[43] *Ephesiaka*,[44] a novel by Xenophon, presents Artemis as being able to preserve, through many trials, two lovers wanting to remain faithful to their vows.[45]

Artemis offered stability that had stood the test of time[46] and so was able to resist the draw to other gods. She prospered during the period 50–150 AD, even increasing in strength and "was well known throughout the world for her goodness and for the success she had bought to Ephesus."[47] The second century saw the educated turning to philosophy and the uneducated turning to Christianity or one of the myriads of new religions, particularly Oriental.[48] These were seen as providing better "answers to human concerns, especially to the crucial question of life after death."[49] Artemis withstood Christianity and was still seen as a rival to it until the fourth century.[50]

Cult Prostitution

Not all accept Artemis as a supporter of chastity, so the presence (or absence) of cult prostitutes in Ephesus has implications for the

40. Strelan, *Paul*, 49.
41. Strabo, *Geogr.* 14.1.20.
42. Strelan, *Paul*, 53.
43. Baugh, "Foreign World," 42.
44. Two of the five preserved Greek novels are centered on Ephesus giving a good look into religion and life in Ephesus.
45. This same concept can be seen in the attempted rape in Achilles Tatius' *Leukippe and Kleitophon*. Achilles Tatius, *Leuc. Clit.* 6.21.2
46. Strelan, *Paul*, 79.
47. Strelan, *Paul*, 80.
48. Knibbe, "Via Sacra," 146.
49. Knibbe, "Via Sacra," 148–49.
50. Strelan, *Paul*, 81.

role of women's ministry in 1 Tim 2:8–15. Sharon Gritz asserts that "undoubtedly some of the new Christian converts had been cultic priestesses"[51] questioning whether the "prominence of the sex-orientated mystery cult of Artemis would prompt a social, though non-Christian acceptability of sexual immorality."[52] The same thought is expressed by Philip Payne who sees the danger of cult prostitutes as providing role models to women in the church.[53]

Cult Prostitution can be defined in two ways:

- Narrowly: union with a prostitute either inside or outside of the temple precinct as a sanctioned act of worship in a fertility ritual. Their status is as semi-official cult functionary; or
- Broadly: it could simply refer to acts of prostitution by slaves owned by the temple where the payment went to a temple and to its administrators.[54]

Cult prostitution is well known outside the Greek world such as in Comana in Pontus.[55] Strabo says, "The temple of Venus at Corinth was so rich, that it had more than a thousand women consecrated to the service of the goddess, courtesans, whom both men and women had dedicated as offerings to the goddess. The city was frequented and enriched by the multitudes who resorted thither on account of these women."[56] His references were to classical times and in his own time there was only a small temple of Venus in Corinth.[57] The practice of cult prostitution was assumed to have taken place in Ephesus based mainly on a reference to the practice in Corinth.[58]

---

51. Gritz, *Paul*, 116.
52. Gritz, *Paul*, 114.
53. Payne, "Liberterian," 183.
54. Baugh, "Cult Prostitution," 444.
55. Strabo, *Geogr.* 12.3.36, 11.14.1. Pontus is centered on the Black Sea.
56. Strabo dates this to the reign of the tyrant Cypselus (657–25 BC). Baugh, "Cult Prostitution," 446; *Strabo, Geogr.* 8.6.20.
57. Strabo, *Geogr.* 8.6.21. Pausanias briefly describes this temple. Pausanias, *Descr.* 2.4.1.
58. Strabo, *Geogr.* 12.3.36.

Cultural and Religious Expectation

Some now confidently assert "cult prostitution did not exist in Ephesus."[59] One researcher states that neither "Strabo, Pliny the Elder, Dio Chrysostom, Pausanias, Xenophon of Ephesus, Achilles Tatius, nor any other ancient author speaks explicitly or even hints at cult prostitution in either the narrow or broad sense in Ephesus of any period. Nor is it evidenced in the nearly 4,000 extant Greek and Latin inscriptions from Ephesus."[60] The references to cult prostitution in Corinth were to Aphrodite, not Demeter, the Greek mother goddess, nor Artemis. In Achilles Tatius' novel, it is clear that Artemis' temple is not like that of Aphrodite as there was no sex there.[61]

Ephesus was a large seaport and prostitution has always been associated with such places. But it seems to be just that, prostitution, not a participation in a fertility rite related to Artemis.

Other Pagan Religions

Despite Ephesus being the cult center for Artemis Ephesia, "a plethora of Greco-Roman and, to a lesser extent, Anatolian deities" were also worshipped.[62] While Rome had been described as the sewer of the Orontes[63] because of the impact of Syrian, Phrygian, and Mithraic religions (frequently associated with very immoral practices), Ephesus remained Greek in its religion despite being an eastern city.[64] Christianity and Egyptian cults were the only ones to make a significant impact in the religious life of Ephesus.[65]

---

59. Baugh, "Cult Prostitution," 444; Freedman, *Anchor Bible Dictionary* 2. 548.
60. Baugh, "Cult Prostitution," 444.
61. Achilles Tatius, *Leuc. Clit.* 5.21.4, 8.10.6.
62. Freedman, *Anchor Bible Dictionary*, 548.
63. Juvenal, *Sat.* 3.60–65.
64. Walters, "Egyptian Religions," 282.
65. Walters, "Egyptian Religions," 282.

Name	Documentation			
	Literature	Coins	Epigraphy	Monuments
Aphrodite	*		*	
Apollo	*	*	*	*
Asclepius	*		*	
Athena	*	*	*	
Cabiri			*	
Demeter	*		*	*
Dionysus	*	*	*	*
Egyptian Cults	*	*	*	*
Ge			*	
God Most High			*	
Hecate	*	*	*	
Hephaestus			*	
Hercules	*	*	*	*
Mother Goddess			*	*
Pluton			*	
Poseidon	*		*	
Zeus	*	*	*	*

Table 1: Evidence of pagan religions[66]

Added to the various pagan religions, select individuals were worshipped, sometimes even while they were alive.

66. Oster, "Ephesus", 548.

Cultural and Religious Expectation

Egyptian Cults

In the third century BC, with the presence of Egyptian merchants and military occupation, the worship of their gods became more prominent in Ephesus. Their worship is known to continue up to the fourth century AD.[67] It is argued that the widespread adoption of Egyptian deities in other cities during the Ptolemies even when there was no occupation may have been motivated more by political considerations.[68] The cult gained prominence in the second century AD, the time of Christian expansion in Ephesus.

Imperial Cult

"*Neokoros*," a term synonymous with the provincial cults, is Latin for "temple warden." The word evolved from referring simply to a temple official through to its benefactor and finally to a city.[69] In Acts 19:35, Ephesus is also called the neokoros of Artemis. The term was unofficial at this stage. A coin from 65/66[70] AD refers to "Neokoros Ephesus," which probably means that the city was the neokoros of Artemis.[71]

During Augustus' time, the temples of Divius Julius and De Roma were built in Ephesus to serve the needs of provincial Romans so making little impact on local Ephesians. Rome was willing, if not anxious, to see Imperial temples established as it wanted to limit the sanctuary role of a Greek temple.[72] Ephesus was first passed over by Pergamum (29 BC)[73] and then by Smyrna (c. 29–35

---

67. Walters, "Egyptian Religions," 304.
68. Walters, "Egyptian Religions," 286.
69. Friesen, "Roman Emperors," 228–29.
70. The only earlier reference to a city calling itself a *neokoros* is Kyzikos in 38 AD. Friesen, "Cult," 231.
71. Friesen, "Roman Emperors," 231.
72. Cornelius Tacitus. *Ann.* 3.60. It is difficult to understand the validity of this argument as the traditional temples did not appear to lose their rights as sanctuaries. It would have curtailed abuses.
73. Cassius Dio, *Rom. His.* 51.20.6.

AD)[74] as the center for the provincial temple mainly because the worship of Artemis was too strong.[75] While there was no Imperial Temple in Ephesus at the time the Pastoral Epistles were written, moves had started to establish one. A fundamental shift in religious thinking was taking place during the time, which would lead to a rearrangement of the hierarchy of the gods. Building on, rather than rejecting the local religious tradition, the emperor would place himself in a direct and superior relationship to Artemis. By the time the Provincial cult was established in Ephesus there were known to be fifty statues to the emperor in the city in which he could be depicted as divine.[76]

The Growing Influence of the Imperial Cult

A temple was eventually built (c. 89–90)[77] in Ephesus for Domitian[78] as *sebastos*,[79] and possibly his wife Domita,[80] along with the other members of the Flavian family, Vespasian and Titus.[81] The temple of Sebastoi was Asia's third operating Imperial temple at a time when all other provinces had only one.[82] In this, Asia was leading the empire in the path of emperor worship.[83] The temple prospered for another century. During Domitian's reign, coins were issued referring to Ephesus as "twice neokoros," i.e., of Artemis and the Sebastoi.[84] It had two dominant and equal cults and

---

74. Friesen, *Twice Neokoros*, 19.
75. Friesen, *Twice Neokoros*, 18.
76. Gill, *Jesus*, 52.
77. Friesen, *Twice Neokoros*, 42.
78. Probably as a result of Domitian's opposition to corrupt Roman governors and starting to reform the tax system. Freisen, *Twice Neokoros*, 158, 160.
79. Literal Greek translation of the Latin term *Augustus*.
80. Friesen, *Twice Neokoros*, 36.
81. Friesen, *Twice Neokoros*, 48.
82. Baugh, "Cult Prostitution," 245.
83. It may well be that Revelation dates from this time and reflects this rise of emperor worship.
84. Friesen, *Twice Neokoros*, 56.

Cultural and Religious Expectation

all the citizens were the protectors of them both.[85] The city was then tied to worship of the emperor, a fundamental shift in how it viewed itself.[86]

Olympian religion[87] was "concerned with the preservation of the ancient ways" and relationships under a proper hierarchy. Temples, games, priesthoods, sacrifices, and reverence were more important than "emotional sincerity, assent to doctrines, or divine essence."[88] For Ephesus, the privilege of hosting the imperial cult would bring prominence in regional affairs, access to the best offices, religious tourists, entertainment, and new revenue streams.[89]

While we have little indication of what the ritual activity entailed,[90] we do know that the Imperial cult was taken seriously. There is no evidence of fulfilled prayer by any emperor, dead or alive,[91] but there are records of intense religious experience (including mysteries performed[92] by priestesses[93]) associated with these gods. In antiquity, all aspects of life, social, religious, economic, and political were intricately intertwined[94] and the emperor's worship was not just political ritual.

The Greeks must surely have seen the inconsistency in saying that Caesar was god while observing he had sacrifices made to other gods. Yet the emperor, in a very visible way, was creating a world pleasing to the gods and so functioned like a god to the Ephesians.[95] The gods in their turn protected the emperor[96] and

---

85. Friesen, *Twice Neokoros*, 57.
86. Baugh, "Cult Prostitution," 236.
87. The principal gods of the Greek Pantheon were believed to live on Mount Olympus.
88. Friesen, *Twice Neokoros*, 166.
89. Friesen, *Twice Neokoros*, 164.
90. Friesen, *Twice Neokoros*, 142.
91. Arnold, *Ephesians*, 37.
92. We do not know what these mysteries were.
93. Harland, *Honours and Worship*, 331.
94. Harland, "Honours and Worship," 322.
95. Friesen, *Twice Neokoros*, 150–53.
96. Friesen, *Twice Neokoros*, 152.

Women in Ministry

the people could show their gratitude and dependence through the cult.[97] Yet the vast majority of evidence equates the emperor with the gods.[98] Certainly "the worship of the emperor was an extension of diplomacy" and "was a way of representing power relationships."[99] In this way, they did not honor the emperor so much as define him.[100]

Women in Ephesian Cults

There is no evidence of women filling senior municipal offices during first-century Ephesus,[101] but it is not the case with religious offices. Considering the Amazon's role in establishing the worship of Artemis Ephesia,[102] it is not surprising that women in Asia Minor were more conspicuous in religious life than elsewhere.[103] In Asia Minor, twenty-eight women are known to have held the position of *pyrtanis* (a position of very high rank involving the finances and cultic life of the city) in eight cities in the first three centuries after Christ, thirty-seven were *stephanephoroi* (positions of high public profile and prestige, if not much political clout) in seventeen cities over a five century period, and eighteen women in fourteen different cities held the position of *agonothetis* (a position of responsibility for contests) in the first three centuries.[104] Still, it must be remembered that "positions open to ten- to fourteen-year-old girls (and boys) did not hold the same social and political

---

97. Friesen, *Twice Neokoros*, 164.

98. E.g., a letter to the Roman proconsul L. Mestrius Florus saying that "mysteries and sacrifices were made to Demeter Karpophoros and Thesmophoros, and to the gods Sebastoi by the initiates in Ephesus every year." Friesen, *Twice Neokoros*, 149.

99. Baugh, "Cult Prostitution," 242.

100. Baugh, "Cult Prostitution," 242.

101. Baugh, "Foreign World," 32.

102. Pausanias, *Descr.* 7.2.4.

103. Strelan, *Paul,* 120.

104. Trebilco, *Jewish Communities,* 120–22.

Cultural and Religious Expectation

authority as held by the Ephesian state council, *gerousia*,[105] or Roman governor."[106] Women only had access to public offices for the first time in the first century AD and would increase in the second and third century.[107]

In Ephesus, women sometimes held the office of priest in their own right without being dependent on their husbands.[108] They were known to be involved in the sacrificial activities from c. 45 AD.[109] Women also served as priestesses in the Artemisia and in the cult of Hestia Boulaia in the civic center. In the Imperial cult, 26 percent of the 138 known high priests were women.[110] They are all understood to have come from wealthy families.[111] This prominent role would not be unnoticed by Ephesian Jews and Christians.

For women, Artemis, who consorted with women and as the huntress took many of the roles that were seen as male, represented life without being constrained by men.[112] The goddess bought the power of women into the realm of men and for men.[113] Greek women's status and honor frequently came with marriage and families, so Artemis' role in preparing maidens for this role was very important.[114]

Demeter, the corn goddess, had a strong following in Ephesus.[115] *Thesmophoria*, a three-day festival exclusive to married women, was intended to "promote the fertility and productivity of

---

105. Baugh describes this influential 300 strong group as the "Old Men's Society." They were respected but their role is uncertain. Baugh, "Foreign World," 33

106. Baugh, "Foreign World," 50.

107. Baugh, "Foreign World," 52, 45.

108. Friesen, *Twice Neokoros*, 84–86; Strelan, *Paul*, 120.

109. Friesen, *Twice Neokoros*, 113.

110. White, "Urban Development," 58.

111. Baugh, "Foreign World," 46.

112. In preparing women for marriage, she would have been seen as advantageous to men also.

113. Strelan, *Paul*, 122.

114. Strelan, *Paul*, 120.

115. Herodotus, *Hist.* 6.16

both women and cereals and to celebrate the procreative qualities of women." During this festival in which the women acted as virgins waiting to be married, "they participated in things excluded to them in normal life."[116] In this festival they could organize a women's society, stay outside overnight, and perform private secret rituals, which included the otherwise forbidden drinking of wine. They even organized women guards to keep the men away.[117] The "wild" nature of this living is in stark contrast to their everyday married life, which was tamed, civilized, and domesticated.

Another cult essentially for women was that of Dionysus who, in Greek mythology, drove the Amazons to find refuge with Artemis in Ephesus. Dionysus made a number of claims similar to Christians. This double god of life and death was both male and female, bringing the power of men into the realm of women.[118] He entered the underworld looking for his mother and came out with the gift of life and celebration.[119] Dionysus was a god of confusion who Achilles Tatius described, along with Apollo, as "the most violent of gods . . . who drives the soul towards madness."[120]

The festival of Dionysius, held in Ephesus's cold winter, turned the city into the wilds outside. The women went about in bare feet and with hair unbraided and ate raw meat and drank wine. All this suggests a trance-like state that climaxed in ecstasy.[121] This possession by the gods was arrived at through chanting, dancing, rhythmic drumming, and cymbals, and the music of flutes.[122] By eating flesh and drinking wine, the participants identified with the god.[123]

The *katagogia* was a festival where the worshippers of Dionysus came down from the hills into the city. Women would come forward to be beaten with cudgels to promote fertility and

---

116. Strelan, *Paul*, 121.
117. Strelan, *Paul*, 121.
118. Strelan, *Paul*, 122.
119. Strelan, *Paul*, 122.
120. Achilles Tatius, *Leuc. Clit.* 2.2.3.
121. Strelan, *Paul*, 122.
122. Strelan, *Paul*, 122.
123. Strelan, *Paul*, 124.

commune with the dead.[124] Death and blood were powerful connections in the cult and in this festival, the participants would "die" and be at one with the god and so access his life-giving power.[125]

Magic in Ephesus

Interest in and fear of supernatural power and the demonic realm gripped the inhabitants of the Hellenistic world in the first century AD. Western Asia Minor was the center of this flourishing magical trade.[126] It is not surprising that in the New Testament book bearing the name Ephesians,[127] there is a strong emphasis on the power of God contrasted with the powers of evil. The Devil and the various powers of evil are mentioned sixteen times.[128] In Acts 19, Luke indicates that there was a substantial number of new Christians who had still been practicing magic. Magic books that were worth 50,000 days wages were burned by the believers.

The spirit world was seen to exercise influence on every aspect of life. The magician's role was to know which spirits were helpful and which were harmful and also to know the operation, strengths, and authority of the spirits.[129] By knowing the right formula, power could be exerted for good, e.g., enhancing sexual passion, or for ill, through uttering a curse. The practitioners of this magic crossed all religious boundaries, calling on a variety of names showing Jewish, Egyptian, and Greek influence.[130] An interest in the divine personalities in the Roman Empire was superseded by an interest in divine power.[131]

---

124. Strelan, *Paul*, 123–24.

125. Strelan, *Paul*, 124.

126. Arnold, *Ephesians*, 5.

127. While there are arguments about who wrote Ephesians and from where, there is strong agreement that the epistle was written to western Asia Minor. It is likely to be a circular letter distributed from Ephesus.

128. Only 1 Corinthians has more references, but it is three times longer.

129. Arnold, *Ephesians*, 18.

130. Arnold, *Ephesians*, 18.

131. Arnold, *Ephesians*, 34.

Women in Ministry

Magic normally differs from religion in two ways:

- It is a deviation from sanctioned religious practice, and
- Its results are almost guaranteed.[132]

As magic was generally practiced by the lower classes, the Egyptian magical papyri [133] give an insight into the beliefs and fears of the common people in the Hellenistic world.[134] The reputation of Ephesus as a magic center is linked to its association with the "Ephesian Letters." These letters, known as early as the fourth century BC, became to be applied to written magical spells. These spells, either as spoken charms or written amulets, were seen to have power to ward off evil spirits.[135] The holder of these names had access to the supernatural power of the being named.

As the *Ephesia Grammata* were written onto Ephesian Artemis' image, her power was given to them and to Hellenistic magic. After studying the magical papyri, Clinton Arnold concludes that "in many instances there seems to be little or no difference between calling on Artemis to accomplish a certain task and utilizing a 'magical' formula. Magic appears to be less a substructure of the cult of Artemis than it is an integral and sanctioned aspect of her 'religion.'"[136] Hellenistic magic in western Asia Minor was not exclusively linked to Artemis though, as all known gods were named in the papyri. There was no real preference for a particular deity.[137]

Astrology was closely associated with magic because through it a person could alter his fate by manipulating the astral powers.

---

132. Arnold, *Ephesians*, 19.

133. The magical documents from Asia Minor have not survived but, due to the dry climate, a number from Egypt have. It is thought that these would be substantially similar to the magic in Asia Minor (Arnold, *Ephesians*, 16). Strelan argues that there is no evidence for this (Strelan, *Paul,* 82). But it does seem reasonable especially as Ephesus was a great port with regular contact with Alexandria.

134. Arnold, *Ephesians*, 20.
135. Arnold, *Ephesians*, 15.
136. Arnold, *Ephesians*, 24.
137. Arnold, *Ephesians*, 35.

Cultural and Religious Expectation

Artemis, with the signs of the zodiac on her image, was unaffected by astrological fate and was able to help her followers and give advice about the future.[138] The mystery religions were closely connected with astrology so accordingly the worship of Artemis Ephesia was also associated with the practice of mysteries. It offered a new way of propitiating the evil heavenly powers.[139] By adding to magic, astrology, and mysteries, the three overlapped to make Artemis's cult very powerful by having complementary ways of manipulating the powers.[140]

Women had influence beyond these cults as well. In Plautus' (third century BC) Latin play, *The Braggard Warrior*, an elderly Ephesian gentleman complained about wives who were always asking their husbands for money to buy presents for their mothers at the matrons' festival (in honor of Mars or possibly Ares) or give to the sorcerer, or dream interpreter, or clairvoyant, or the soothsayer.[141] Each term is female and each woman charged for their services.

Gnosticism

Ephesus was a center for early Gnosticism, a speculative religious belief that would plague the second-century church. Gnosticism was set in the framework of contemporary philosophy, mythology and astrology, and later Christianity. At Gnosticism's core was the "mystery religions which mediate secret knowledge leading to salvation and from magic whose knowledge confers supernatural powers and union with God."[142] Apart from philosophy, the strong, and at times, leading role of women in these areas has been noted. This was not a unified belief but comprised many competing groups with very different teachings, which included how Eve

---

138. Arnold, *Ephesians*, 28.
139. Arnold, *Ephesians*, 29.
140. Arnold, *Ephesians*, 29.
141. Bultmann, "γινώσκω", 1.691–99.
142. Bultmann, "γινώσκω", 1.692–93.

was presented. She could be portrayed as preceding Adam and even giving him life and teaching him.[143]

It is disputed whether this heresy actually existed in its full-blown form in the first century and scholars generally refer to proto-Gnosticism during this period.[144] Because of Gnostic tendencies that existed in the first century, a limited agreement has developed between those who accept and those who deny Pauline authorship of the Pastoral Epistles.[145] The heresy in the Pastorals is said to be at least an early form of Gnosticism originating in Christians with a Hellenistic Jewish background, which merged the associated beliefs into orthodox Christianity. There are also close similarities with the Hellenistic Judaism found in Colossae (Col 2:3–8, 16–23). Mixing Christianity with pagan elements was a present danger and, we will see in the next chapter, a consideration for the writer of First and Second Timothy.

This heresy was sufficiently developed by the time the Apostle John lived in Ephesus and of such a danger that Irenaeus stated that John's gospel was written to refute an early proponent, Cerinthus.[146] Polycarp (a disciple of John and teacher of Irenaeus) told the story of John "going to bathe at Ephesus, and perceiving Cerinthus within, rushed out of the bath-house without bathing, exclaiming, 'Let us fly, lest even the bath-house fall down, because Cerinthus, the enemy of the truth, is within.'"[147]

Judaism

The religious scene represented by Table 1 presents a very confusing religious setting. The Greeks and Romans had no problem worshipping one then another of the Greek or Roman pantheon or for that matter even participating in totally different, unrelated

---

143. E.g., MacRae, "Apocalypse of Adam," and Wisse, "Apocryphon of John."

144. Arnold, *Ephesians*, 9.

145. Towner, "Gnosis," 96.

146. Irenaeus, "Against Heresies," 3.11.1.

147. Irenaeus, "Against Heresies," 3.3.4.

Cultural and Religious Expectation

religions. Only the Jews, initially, stood apart from all this. Christianity and Judaism were different through demanding the sole allegiance of the believer to their God.

Jews lived in Ephesus from the early Hellenistic period[148] and their numbers strengthened after Antiochus III moved two thousand Jewish families from Mesopotamia to Asia Minor to secure his hold there.[149] The population remained large during the Roman period. Despite not having formal citizenship, there were collective rights enjoyed by the community.[150] Their most probable status was of *isopoliteia*, i.e., potential citizenship that could only be validated by participation in the pagan rites.[151]

Josephus shows that the community of Jews in Asia Minor maintained concern for matters at the heart of their faith and protected their Jewish identity. They were known to have built synagogues and the sanctity of their scriptures was ensured by Rome.[152] There was continued loyalty to Jerusalem and the temple worship. The temple tax was granted the same sanctity as a pagan temple,[153] and was paid by every male and shipped to Jerusalem. The observance of the Sabbath by the Jews was very strong and conscientious.[154] The decree to Sardis[155] stipulated that the city was to ensure that suitable food was to be available to the Jews indicating that the Jews of Asia Minor were able to satisfy their food laws.

The Greeks were intolerant of both a religious system that was very strange to them[156] and for the special privileges the Jews experienced. There was also political anti-Semitism manifested by the Greek cities of Asia in the second half of the first century.[157] The

---

148. Josephus, *C. Ap.* 2.29.
149. Safrai and Stern, *Jewish People*, vol. 1, 152.
150. Safrai and Stern, *Jewish People*, vol. 1, 439.
151. Safrai and Stern, *Jewish People*, vol. 1, 438.
152. Josephus, *A.J.* 16.6.2.
153. Josephus, *A.J.* 16.2.4, 16.6.2.
154. Josephus, *A.J.* 14.10.24.
155. Josephus, *A.J,* 14.10.24
156. Josephus, *A.J.* 16.2.4.
157. Safrai and Stern, *Jewish People*, vol. 1, 668.

Women in Ministry

profitable trade in luxury goods coming from Africa via the Red Sea or the Orient and Arabia via Petra,[158] came through Judean harbors, presumably with Jewish middlemen. Despite opposition, the Jew's religion in Asia Minor was protected by the Selucids[159] and later the Romans.[160] Their rights were accepted and defined on an ad hoc basis.[161]

Unfortunately, this privilege was directed toward men. This was not always the case in Judaism as there was a positive image of women in Wisdom literature and through people such as Deborah who led men (Judg 4:4–24) and the married prophetess, Huldah who taught men (2 Chron 34:19–28). After the exile there was a fundamental shift to reduce women's participation. Herod's temple had a court for the women, something that did not exist in the tabernacle or Solomon's temple. They could now be grouped with children and slaves.[162]

There are occasional references to women knowing the law,[163] but normally they were only allowed to hear, not to learn.[164] Learning was an extravagance likened to learning "sexual satisfaction."[165] Women were exempted from participating in the rituals and feasts.[166] Though they could say a benediction over a meal for their husband,[167] they could not ask someone to say it for them.[168] They

---

158. Safrai and Stern, *Jewish People*, vol. 1, 482.

159. Josephus, *A.J.* 14.10.22.

160. Josephus, *A.J.* 14.10.23–25; 16.6.1.

161. Josephus, *A.J.* 14.10.8; 16.6.1–7.

162. E.g., Mishna *Ber.* 3:3, *Sukkah* 2:8, *Roš Ha*, 1:8.

163. Babylonian Talmud *'Erub.* 53b–54a; *Ketub.* 23a; Mishna. *Šabb.* 6:1; *Sota* 3:4

164. Babylonian Talmud *Hagigah* 3a.

165. Mishna, *Soṭah* 3:4, cf. Babylonian Talmud, *Soṭah*. 21b. The reasoning was that by having merit through learning the Torah, should a woman commit adultery she will avoid, at least for a time, the effect of the test for adultery in Num 5:11–31.

166. E.g., Mishna *Sukkah* 2:8; *Ber.* 3:3.

167. Babylonian Talmud *Sukkah* 38a.

168. Mishna, *Ber.* 7:2.

Cultural and Religious Expectation

were not even permitted to teach children.[169] In short, a woman's role was not honored and she would have had a low expectancy for any ministry role had she stayed in Judaism.

Mixed Expectations around Ministry

Women had a vastly different experience and expectation from their participation in the different pagan religions and in Judaism. Those women coming from religions that accepted active involvement in paganism are not likely to willingly accept restrictions in the roles already enjoyed. Through participation in the intense religious experiences, there was something approaching, at times, full equality of sexes in a religious setting at least. On the other hand, many Jewish men were not likely to desire any changes to the very subordinate position they had placed on women. This repression is likely to be especially entrenched in a city where strong independent women of mythology were revered, and a female deity was worshipped with the aid of priestesses. A church made of Jewish and formerly pagan believers is likely to have experienced great tension with some women seeking continued participation, some clamoring for freedom, and some men having an entrenched disposition toward suppression.

If this wasn't enough for Paul and Timothy to deal with in Ephesus, it was further complicated by the false teachers whose beliefs will be explored in the next chapter. There we will see that it was likely that some believed a time had been ushered in where all the blessings of God's future kingdom were already realized. With that came the dawning of an age when the women had true equality with men, as marriage with its respective roles no longer should exist.

---

169. Mishna, *Qidd.* 4:13.

2

The Ephesian Heresy
and Ministry Roles

PAUL'S LETTERS TO TIMOTHY and Titus are not theological treatises like Romans that float free of time and circumstances. Nor, in my opinion, is it correct to see these letters as manuals for church order that have no constraints and apply equally to all churches in all nations in all time periods. It is better to see them as ad hoc letters to close friends who needed to address circumstances in specific churches at a given time. The stated purpose for writing, at least with First Timothy, was to protect the faith of the Ephesian believers from the attacks they were encountering (1 Tim 1:3) and to instruct believers how they should behave (1 Tim 3:14–15), presumably as a consequence of that attack. That is far from saying they are irrelevant and that everything was focused on a long forgotten false teaching that had to be countered roughly two thousand years ago. Still, a modern reader needs to consider what was situational and what is fixed. This chapter looks at the nature of the heresy that was encountered and how that is likely to have impacted the pattern of church government Paul would introduce. I believe that this pattern was changing as the church matured, became more organized and had to address its continued existence after the Apostles had died.

The Ephesian Heresy

The restriction of women's ministry in First and Second Timothy is very likely related to their involvement in the heresy Timothy had to confront. However, determining what exactly the heresy was has proven difficult, if not impossible.[1] Paul addressed the character failings[2] of the false teachers, not the heresy itself. This lack of consensus among scholars about the nature of what they taught gives rise to even more theories,[3] making it virtually impossible to say what the women believed and what role they played in disrupting the church.

While the doctrines promoted by the heretics were not Christian, we are struck more with its futility than its error, so much so that Paul only denounced it and did not bother to refute it.[4] Timothy, an experienced Christian worker, was more than capable of that.[5] Donald Guthrie says its danger was "not so much in falseness as its irrelevance."[6] Their teachings were foolish controversies based on no more than speculations over myths and genealogies. Their disputes about the Law were useless (2 Tim 2:14), unprofitable, and worthless (Titus 3:9).

Yet this heresy is presented not as the misguided imagination of ill-informed teachers, but the doctrine of demons (1 Tim 4:1)

---

1. The nature of the heresy is expanded upon in this author's *Introduction to the Pastoral Epistles*.
2. The six areas addressed are teaching for financial reward (1 Tim 6:5; Titus 1:11), deception (2 Tim 3:13), hypocrisy (2 Tim 3:5; Titus 1:16; 3:8–9), arguing over words not substance (1 Tim 1:4, 6; 4:2; 2 Tim 2:14, 16, 23; Titus 1:10; 3:9), various vices (1 Tim 1:9–10; 2 Tim 3:2–4), and success among women (2 Tim 3:6).
3. Young, *Theology*, 3.
4. Guthrie, *New Testament Introduction*, 628–29.
5. Guthrie, *New Testament Introduction*, 629.
6. Guthrie, *New Testament Introduction*, 628.

and so was insidious. The danger of this heresy could be seen in its outworking of strife (Titus 3:9), the way it caused quarrels (2 Tim 2:23), and ultimately leading to ruin (2 Tim 2:14). The Pauline virtues of faith, hope, and love appear to be in short supply in the arrogant (2 Tim 3:2), argumentative, and divisive false teachers (Titus 1:11; 3:9–11).

It is difficult to see how Paul's teaching on the equality of men and women before God could allow the continuation of the cultural subjection of women to a life of servitude, repression, and ignorance. The message of emancipation was at least implicit in Paul's teaching as he had advised slaves to gain their freedom if they could (1 Cor 7:21) and encouraged women to be taught the faith (1 Tim 2:11). This hope of emancipation must have received a welcome among many of the oppressed as they reflected on the implications of Paul's teaching. Unfortunately, without moral character and wisdom in some of its leaders, it appears not to have been held in balance. It is quite likely that this radical aspect of Paul's gospel was seized upon by the heretics resulting in the disruption of the normal social structure in the home and church. David Mappes describes the conduct in the church as "slaves disobeyed masters; women usurped the role of men in the church as women were emancipated from the traditional domination of their husbands, and widows became attracted to an aesthetic lifestyle."[7]

If correct, this then would not be a gradual outworking but a revolution! The resurrection was passed, it was claimed (2 Tim 2:18), suffering had passed, and this was a time of reigning with Christ.[8] Such a radical expression of Christianity would have made the church a pariah in the Ephesian society. Very likely, over time, the ultimate outworking of emancipation would have seen the attempted removal of the final shackle—the political chains of Rome. The events of the Jewish revolt would demonstrate how perilous that would have been for the church. Salvation in the Pastoral Epistles is a past (2 Tim 1:9; Titus 3:5), present (1 Tim 1:15; 4:8), and future (1 Tim 4:8, 16; 2 Tim 4:18) event. For the heretics

7. Mappes, "Heresy," 459.
8. Mappes, "Heresy," 458.

The Ephesian Heresy and Ministry Roles

who believed the resurrection had passed, it was only a past and present event. Perhaps the difference between freedom and salvation had been blurred. There is an association, but as Aida Spencer observes, freedom needs an understanding of its nature otherwise it can develop into a parody of that very liberation, which would lead to another form of slavery.[9]

A church that was settling into a period before Christ's re-appearing had time to change society and had time to set its priorities. Paul prevented the Ephesian church from moving in the radical direction of the heretics and could have found it expedient to have backed down on the role of women.[10] But elsewhere, Paul argued that there should not have been a gap between theory and practice as he strongly criticized Peter for discriminating between Jew and Gentile (Gal 2:11–14).[11] What would Paul do in a modern church that discriminates between men and women?

Some of those who were taking the church into error were its own leaders (Acts 20:30; 1 Tim 1:3, 7; 6:3). This was different from Galatia and Corinth where the problems were caused by outsiders (Gal 2:4, cf. 2 Cor 11:4). The danger of these teachers was the greater because of their association with Paul, which gave them credibility (Acts 19–20). It is expected that at this stage the church in Ephesus was based on home churches, each presumably with at least one elder. The impact on the Ephesian church, most likely, would not be so much a matter of splitting a congregation into two groups but instead be one of complete home churches departing. Some of these churches may have been held in the homes of widows who were uneducated about life and the faith (2 Tim 3:6). The family provided the model for church leadership and so any threat to the household was a threat to the institution.[12]

The over-realized eschatology of Corinth may also have arisen from a misinterpretation of Paul's teaching that believers have been raised with him and will share in his reign (Rom 6:3–8; Eph 2:5; Col

---

9. Spencer, "Eve at Ephesus," 220.
10. Similarly, Spencer, "Eve at Ephesus," 220.
11. Spencer, "Eve at Ephesus," 220.
12. Young, *Theology*, 39.

2:12, cf. 2 Tim 2:12). This view saw believers expecting in this era much, if not all, of what was to be anticipated in the next. This may have been especially attractive to women. Rather than seeing salvation as a process, the enthusiasts thought they had already experienced the transformation that was to come. This belief likely led to the strange behavior we see pictured in the city's home churches.

The step from "realized eschatology to emancipatory activism"[13] is small and logical. The effect seen in Corinth may illuminate the situation in Ephesus. Paul's teaching had stated that social, racial, and sexual divisions were nothing in the community of faith (Gal 3:28; Col 3:11; 1 Cor 12:13). Consequently, the Corinthian women were upsetting the balance in the community (1 Cor 11:2–16; 14:33–35). If not already active, it was at least an anticipated probability that their attitude would spread to the slaves (1 Cor 7:17–24). Paul wrote to the church attempting to bring the enthusiasts' equality back into balance. Three times he advised the groups in the church to stay as they are (1 Cor 7:17, 20, 24).

The author of the Pastorals was concerned about social balance as well as the heresy and we see very similar themes addressed in the Pastorals as in First Corinthians. Here in Ephesus, women and slaves were also causing problems in the church. The women are told to dress appropriately (1 Tim 2:9) and were limited in their authority over men[14] (1 Tim 2:9–15). Slaves were commanded to respect and obey their masters (1 Tim 6:1–2, cf. Titus 2:9–10). There may also have been problems in the family (1 Tim 2:15; 3:4–5, 12; 5:4, 8, 16; Titus 2). Can the social problems be related to the heresy (1 Tim 1:20; 2 Tim 2:17)?

There is some understanding of the heretics' methods. They were finding openings in the household—upsetting whole households in the process (2 Tim 3:6; Titus 1:11). Many women were targeted, and some were succumbing to the heresy (2 Tim 3:6; 1 Tim 5:15), but it was not only women who accepted the teaching as its ringleaders were men. These men, deceived by demons, were equated to the worst sinners of the end times. They could no longer

13. Towner, "Gnosis," 99.
14. Refer to the next chapter for a discussion on this very difficult passage.

see that their motive was greed (Titus 1:11; 1 Tim 6:5, 9) as their conscience was seared (1 Tim 4:1–2). This is different language from that used of the women. The view of feminine evil where women are weak,[15] more impressionable and impulsive than men, and so much more likely to sin than men, cannot be supported by this and other passages in the Pastorals. These were not the powerful women held in high regard by the New Testament writers and they are not called weak but "little, silly women."[16] While these women probably disseminated the teaching, it was men, Hymenaeus, Philetus, and Alexander, who led the heresy.

Teaching of emancipation must have been attractive to women in a city with its founding associated with the Amazons and the prominent roles given to some women including at the temple of Artemis Ephesia and soon to come in the imperial cult. The desire for emancipation without obedience and responsibility is stifled and Paul calls the women of both Corinth and Ephesus back to "the culturally acceptable role and conduct of women"[17] (1 Tim 2:8–15; 1 Cor 14:33–35). It is understandable if young widows might not want to marry, seeing "Christian widowhood as the best means of independence from marriage and family life."[18] It was a deeper issue though than just independence as they were neglecting to support their own mothers (1 Tim 5:16)[19] and instead supported the heretical teachers. Also wanting was modesty in attire, which was a Greco-Roman virtue in women.[20] The advice on what not to wear (1 Tim 2:9) shows these women were wealthy and, presumably, more likely to have home churches and want leadership roles.[21] That does not mean that they were educated or of high rank

---

15. Words used to translate the "silly women" of the NRSV are "weak willed" RSV and "weak" NASB.
16. Gritz, *Paul*, 111.
17. Towner, "Gnosis," 111.
18. Padgett, "Wealthy Women," 21.
19. This neglect of parents can be seen in Hansen, "Acts of Paul," 43.
20. Padgett, "Wealthy Women," 23.
21. Padgett, "Wealthy Women," 23.

or status in society and may mean no more than their husbands were commercially successful.

Where did the restrictions on marriage originate (1 Tim 4:3, cf. Titus 2:4–5)? Prohibitions on marriage was a part of some form of Gnosticism but this was also a feature of the Essenes/Qumran covenanters[22] and was also present in Corinth. The view among some in Corinth and Ephesus that Christ's return had passed would have been enough to explain the prohibition of marriage in both cities. Marriage in the new order would be unspiritual and the teaching of Jesus himself could be used as support. In the coming kingdom women will no longer marry or be given in marriage (Matt 22:30). The belief that the resurrection had passed, with its implications for an over realized eschatology, could produce opposite effects just as Gnosticism could produce opposite effects. Corinth, which appeared to be free of a Judaizing influence, produced liberty while in Ephesus it was restraint.

We know that many of the early members had participated in the city's religions as many had practiced magic, and magic scrolls worth 50,000 days wages were burned by them (Acts 19:19). These people, who had not lived blameless lives (Acts 19:18), would also be familiar with the intense religious experiences offered in the mysteries of the pagan religions surrounding them. This intense encounter and participation was open to women. It would only have been a short jump to attempt to Hellenize Christianity into a religious experience where a shell of Christian terminology was present but without its vital core of exclusive and ethical truth.

Opinion of Unbelievers

Paul is very concerned about the opinion that society in general had of the believers and throughout the Pastoral Epistles, each group is called to exemplary behavior. Elders had to be well thought of by outsiders and disgrace was to be avoided as it was not just "losing face" but the snare of the devil (1 Tim 3:7). The older women were to

---

22. Towner, "Gnosis," 108.

train the young women in their responsibilities as wives and mothers, "so that the word of God will not be dishonored" (Titus 2:5 NASB). Similarly, young widows were to "give the enemy no opportunity for slander" (1 Tim 5:14 NASB). How Christian this behavior was has been questioned by some. James Walters asserts that "Christianity no longer looked upon itself as a religious sect with a divine calling that required commitment to unusual ethical demands. Rather, the church had become obligated to the world and society at large and had to fulfill the general social norms in an exemplary fashion."[23] The Australian Royal Commission to Institutional Responses to Child Sexual Abuse has laid bare the peril of the church putting its reputation above the insistence of matching behavior.

The lives of young men were to be a "model of good works" and their faith seen through "soundness of speech that cannot be condemned, so that those who oppose you may be ashamed because they have nothing bad to say about us" (Titus 2:8 NASB). Despite their lowly social status, Christian slaves were not exempt, and they also must be held in high regard so "the name of God and the teaching may not be blasphemed" (1 Tim 6:1). This respect could not be earned if they did not hold their masters in high regard. Their good service and honesty would show this respect "so that in every way they will make the teaching about God our Savior attractive." (Titus 2:10 NASB)

Paul taught that "the grace of God has appeared that offers salvation to all people" (Titus 2:11 NASB). There was an equality that cut across every social and sexual division that existed in the city. This radical equality was open to great abuse (1 Tim 6:2) and would work against the church if there was not an accompanying equality "in the high standard of Christian character and intercourse in the church as the family of God."[24] Permeating this call to develop Christian character is the expectation that the church would be a teaching community in which all were involved. Elders were teaching the church, old women were to teach what is good, not just in their family but to the young wives. Young men were to

---

23. Walters, "Egyptian Religions," 302.
24. Lock, *Pastoral*, 3.

Women in Ministry

teach with integrity and gravity (Titus 2:6). Only slaves were not mentioned as having a teaching role.

Purpose of Ministry in the Pastoral Epistles

Purpose of the Ministry of Timothy and Titus

Under the Ignatian style episcopal system, Timothy and Titus would be seen as acting as a Metropolitan, over the Ephesian and Cretan community, respectively.[25] There is, however, no evidence to see them as anything other than apostolic delegates, representing the Apostle Paul to the Gentiles.[26] They were fulfilling a role like the ones they already exercised during their ministry in Macedonia and Achia.[27] Arguing against the monarchical episcopate was Paul's failure to mention that only one elder (bishop) was to be appointed in each church as the term "bishop" was used indiscriminately with elders. The responsibility of a church (or home church) did not rest with an individual but a group. Apart from Phil 1:1, there is no other supporting reference to the titles "overseers" and "deacons," and this verse gives no indication of their actual duties. It does, however, show that plural leadership was not unique to Ephesus and Crete. Paul also gave no instruction about how to perpetuate this role.

Paul had shown what it was to minister with a clear conscience and behavior that was above reproach. Fee observes that Timothy and Titus were not put forward to show us what a pastor is like.[28] In Paul's absence, both Timothy and Titus were to again provide proper examples of what Christ was like (1 Tim 4:12; Titus 2:7–8). This role was especially important when there were now competing

---

25. Evidence for this is that they received their authority at ordination, were of higher rank than the elders, appointed and disciplined elders, and they are responsible for instruction and discipline. Guthrie, *Pastoral*, 30.

26. Guthrie, *New Testament Introduction*, 627.

27. Guthrie, *New Testament Introduction*, 627.

28. Fee, *1 and 2 Timothy*, 147.

The Ephesian Heresy and Ministry Roles

voices as to who represented Christ. Today, can women, as part of a similar group, provide clear examples of what Christ is like?

Purpose of the Recognized Church Offices

From the start of his mission trips, Paul was concerned about good governance in the churches. With the established and proven pattern of governance in the synagogue as a guide, Paul appointed elders at the earliest possibility (Acts 14:23). Elders were known to have been established early in the church in Ephesus (Acts 20:17). Surprisingly, in the universally acknowledged Pauline epistles, there is very little reference to the officers of the church.[29] In the Ephesian epistle, it refers to pastors and teachers which approximate the roles we encounter in the Pastorals. Depending on how we assess the historicity of the Pastorals will determine whether the ecclesiastical setting presented in them is just an anachronism or an apostolic model. Some would see the early church as a charismatic and Spirit infused organism that avoided formal structure for over fifty years.[30]

There was no obstacle to sophisticated church government occurring during Paul's lifetime. Organization would have been essential as the church progressed from having a developing tradition guided by apostolic witness to local leaders who were tradition bearers, (e.g., 2 Tim 2:2; Titus 1:9).[31] Paul's directions seemed less about organizing the church and more about reforming it.[32] The churches, with an emphasis on charisma, had proven to be fraught with problems.[33] An ill-disciplined charismatic membership in Corinth had caused major problems and now ill-disciplined elders

---

29. Leading to the suggestion that the Acts references are anachronistic. Guthrie, *New Testament Introduction*, 625.

30. Von Campenhausen, *Ecclesiastical Authority*, 76–123.

31. Guthrie, *Pastoral*, 29.

32. Fee, *1 and 2 Timothy*, 147.

33. Views that see problems with the church organization in the Pastorals generally invoke special pleading by expunging from Acts the references to Paul and Barnabas appointing elders. Guthrie, *Pastoral*, 27.

were leading the church astray in Ephesus. Yet even in Corinth, there were believers with the spiritual gift of administration (1 Cor 12:28). Secular organizational skills were sophisticated enough to run an empire stretching from Britain to Egypt. In Ephesus, the Apostle was friends with the Asiarchs (Acts 19:31) who organized large games at a time when Ephesus was "crowded to capacity with hordes of people from all over Ionia."[34] It is difficult to imagine that there was not enough skill to organize a church when they had the model of the synagogue and a large family to follow! The heresy had made them acutely aware of what problems they had to confront.

Church government is different in First Timothy to that in Titus. Paul had spent an extended period in Ephesus, sufficient time to develop a structure with overseers and deacons. Yet despite Paul's regular teaching, many of them simply had not learned the gospel.[35] Poor leadership had allowed the false teachers to develop a strong foothold. Establishing a functioning church government was critical in Ephesus and twenty seven of the 113 verses of First Timothy deal with this.[36] In Crete, which appears to be a much younger church, only elders were appointed without deacons (Titus 1:5). This suggests that deacons were only appointed after the church grew. Church government was much less an issue as it was only the subject of five verses out of forty-six in Titus.

It has been observed that for the officers in the church:

- Their qualifications were primarily moral as the behavior of the officer should validate the message he brings,
- The officers were seen sometimes as servants and other times as members of God's household, and
- The actual requirements of and interplay between different members in a household (e.g., slave, mother, father, elderly, and young) applied metaphorically to the church officers.[37]

---

34. Barclay, *Ambassador*, 119.
35. Mounce, *Pastoral Epistles*, lvii.
36. Mounce, *Pastoral Epistles*, lix.
37. Pietersen, *Polemic*, 98–99.

The Ephesian Heresy and Ministry Roles

The formalized lists of virtues and vices seen in the Pastoral Epistles are unlike anything in the Old Testament. There are short lists of vices (Prov 6:17–19; Jer 7:9; Hos 4:2), but perhaps there is little need to list the virtues as the Covenant, either in its concentrated form or in the myriad of laws, required a universal high standard for priest and laity alike. Because of this difference, some see these lists as representing Hellenistic, rather than biblical values. It is claimed they are no more than a "floating list of vices currently available and easily adaptable to the writer's purpose, a whiplash of stringing words of the sort that any orator of the time well understood where to get and how to use."[38] This view would make these lists no more than an attempt to gain respectability and peace in a pagan world.[39] However, Paul made a habit of making virtue and vice lists in which Christian content was put in Hellenistic paraenetic form.[40]

It is possible that Paul was aware of the numerous parallels in pagan,[41] Christian,[42] and Jewish[43] sources. A close similarity is claimed[44] with the description of a general in Onsander's *Stratego*.[45] The comparison between the ideal general and the ideal elder is not surprising. The church was seen at war (Eph 6:10–17; 1 Tim 1:18; 2 Tim 2:3) and the elders as its generals, with God the Commander in Chief.

In the qualifications for office bearers, there was no mention of the possession of the Spirit, (cf., Acts 6:3) or of the intellectual capacity of the office bearers. These two characteristics, desirable

---

38. Gealy, "First," 498.

39. Dibelius and Conzelmann, *Pastoral*, 8–10, 39, 14.

40. Where the hearer is reminded of something he already knows. Gordon, "James," 109–10.

41. Diogenes, *Laertius* VII 116ff.

42. Polycarp, *Epistle to the Philippians*.

43. E.g., Rule 4 of the *Rule of the Community* has no mention of women.

44. Two of the eleven words in Onsander's list are the same as Paul's list and three are similar, but the dissimilarities are so striking that it is hard to argue dependence Mappes, "Moral Virtues," 212.

45. Onsander, *Stratego* 1:2–17 (C. AD 58).

as they are, are very hard to measure objectively and may well have been deliberately omitted by Paul. The clear evidence of the possession of the Spirit as seen in the original deacons was now muddied. The "possession" of the Spirit in Corinth was no longer a reliable sign of true spirituality. Cleverness alone was no sign of fitness for office as a false intellectualism was taking the Ephesian church into heresy.

Paul was establishing a framework based on imitation but were the requirements for office simply striving for middle class respectability based on imitating a Hellenistic standard?[46] The model clearly did have similarities with the Hellenistic virtues, but there is nothing in the Pastorals that show the ethic of the church had changed. This ethic was one of difference and change leading to severance from paganism on one hand and from gross Christian error on the other. This framework was one whereby true spirituality and possession of true knowledge could be judged. This was found not in copying the best of the Hellenistic world, but through the imitation of the example of trusted officers. In a sense, the guidelines are qualifications, not to be a ruler, but to be a role model. A smaller church than that at Ephesus may have little need of administrators, but the requirement for a role model remained crucially important.

The primary function of church officers as models of Christ, as indeed it was in First Timothy and Titus, could be fulfilled equally by males and females. This is established in Table 2 that follows. This is a distinct advance on Judaism as practiced at the time of the church's establishment. While we normally understand men as filling these roles, the question is whether they were ever filled by women as a recognized office rather than unofficially.

Qualifications for Church Office

The qualifications for church office from the Pastoral Epistles are listed in table form below. What is important to notice is that

46. Mappes, "Moral Virtues," 208.

The Ephesian Heresy and Ministry Roles

every role required of the elders has a matching requirement for all women.

Episkopoi in 1 Timothy 3	*Diakonoi* in 1 Timothy 3	*Presbyteroi* in Titus 1	All Women in 1 Timothy	Nature
v1 They desire a good work, *kalou ergou*			2:10 Adorn themselves... with good works, *ergōn agathōn*; 5:10 Devoted herself to every good work *ergois kalois*	
1. General Requirements—All Positive				
(1) Christian Morality in General				
(a) v2 Above reproach, unassailable, *anepilēmpton*	v8 Worthy of respect	v6 Must be blameless	5:7 above reproach, *anepilēmptoi*	Moral
(b) v2 Married once, *mias gynaikos andra*	Married once	v6 Husband of one wife	5:9 married once, *henos andros gynē*	Moral
(c) v2 Temperate, *nēphalion*			3:11 temporate *nēphalious*	Moral
(d) v2 Self control, *sōphrona*		v7 Not quick tempered; v8, self controlled	2:9, 15 self control, *sōphrosynēs*	Moral
(e) v2 Respectable *kosmion*	v8 Sincere	v8 loves what is good	2:9 respectable, *kosmiō*	Moral

39

Women in Ministry

Episkopoi in 1 Timothy 3	*Diakonoi* in 1 Timothy 3	*Presbyteroi* in Titus 1	All Women in 1 Timothy	Nature
(2) Morality in Relation to the Church				
(a) v2 Hospitable *philoxenon*		v8 Hospitable	5:10 Entertained strangers, given relief to the oppressed *exenodochēsen, thlibomenois epērkesen*	Spiritual
(b) v2 Able to teach *didaktikon*	v9 Hold the deep truths with a clear conscience	v9 Hold deep truths so he can encourage and refute	2:10 Let learn *manthanetō*, cf. 1:7 (Some are) teachers of the law *nomodidaskaloi* cf. Titus 2:3 Teachers of what is good, *kalodidaskalous*	Spiritual
2. Detailed Requirements—Mainly Negative				
(1) In daily life				
(a) v3 Little wine, *mē paroinon*	v8 Little wine	v7 Not given to drunkenness	3:11 Temporate *nēphalious*, cf. Titus 2:3 Not enslaved to much wine, *mē oinō pollō dedoulōmenas*	Moral
(b) v3 Not violent but gentle, *mē plēktēn alla epieikē*		v7 Not overbearing	2:15 Love, holiness, and self-restraint, *agapē kai. hagiasmō, sōphrosynēs*; 3:11 Not slanderers, *mē diabolous*, cf. Titus 3:2 (For all) peaceable, *amachous*	Moral
(c) v3 Not quarrelsome, *amachon*		v7 Not violent	3:11 Not slanderers, *mē diabolous*, cf. Titus 3:2 (for all) *amachous*	Moral

The Ephesian Heresy and Ministry Roles

Episkopoi in 1 Timothy 3	*Diakonoi* in 1 Timothy 3	*Presbyteroi* in Titus 1	All Women in 1 Timothy	Nature
(2) In Relation to the Church				
(a) v3 Not a lover of money *aphilargyron*	v8 No dishonest gain	v7 Not pursuing dishonest gain	2:9 Not [with] gold, pearls or costly clothing, *mē... chrysiō ē margaritais ē himatismō polytelei*; 3:11 faithful in all things, *pistas en pasin*; 6:10 (For all) Not [having] love of money, *[mē] philargyria*	Moral
(b) v4 manages his house and children with dignity, *tou idiou oikou kalōs proistameno tekna echonta en hypotagē meta pasēs semnotētos*	v12 Manages his household	v6 Children who believe	5:14 Manage their household, *oikodespotein* cf. Eph 6:1–2; 5:14 To bear children and manage their household. *teknogonein oikodespotein*; 3:11 (with) dignity, *semnas*	Moral
(c) v6 Not a recent convert, *mē neophyton*	v10 must first be tested	v8 Holy	5:11 [Not] younger, *[mē] neōteras*, cf. 2:15; 5:5, 9	Spiritual
(d) v6 Not proud, *mē typhōtheis*			2:9 (Dressed in) respectable apparel with modesty... not with costly clothing, *en katastolē kosmiō meta aidous... mē himatismō polytelei*; 2:11 In all submissiveness, *en pasē hypotagē*; 5:10 She has washed feet, *podas enipsen*	

Women in Ministry

Episkopoi in 1 Timothy 3	*Diakonoi* in 1 Timothy 3	*Presbyteroi* in Titus 1	All Women in 1 Timothy	Nature
(e v7 Good reputation with those outside, *kai martyrian kalēn echein apo tōn exōthen*		v8 Upright	3:11 *(with) dignity, semnas*	Moral
(4) The Consequences of Failure				
(a v6 receive same penalty as Devil, *eis krima empesē tou diabolou*			5:12 Judgment, *krima*; 5:15 *exetrapēsan opisō tou satana*	
(b v7 Fall into disgrace, *mē eis oneidismon empesē*			5:14–15 Not allowing reproach from those opposing, *[mē] didonai tō antikeimenō loidorias*	
(c v7 Fall into the Devil's trap *kai pagida tou diabolou*			5:14–15 Because [some] have already turned aside after Satan, *charin . . . exetrapēsan opisō tou satana*	

Table 2. Qualifications of church office[47]

From Table 2 it is clear that each of the overseer descriptions applied to women as well. Payne calculates the mathematical odds for the linguistic similarity happening by pure chance (without taking into account any of the other parallels using different terminology) are approximately one in 300 quintillion.[48]

47. Modified from Payne, "Liberterian," 194.
48. Payne, "Liberterian," 194–95. He puts the odds at 6 in one million if

Formal Church Offices

A brief overview of the formal ministry roles presented in the Pastoral Epistles is helpful in understanding the areas of possible ministry for women in First and Second Timothy. But first, consider how office bearers could be installed in the religious office at the Artemisium and in public office. As was normal in Hellenist cities, civil magistrates exercised control of the temple and Roman governors meddled in their affairs.[49] Baugh quotes an inscription from 44 AD from the provincial proconsul Pallus Fabius Persicus, which includes:

> While using the appearance of the divine temple as a pretext, they sell the priesthoods as if at public auction. Indeed, they invite men of every kind to their sale, then they do not select the most suitable men upon whose head the crown would fittingly be placed.[50]

The other way to positions of power was through patronage, or good works, a system with "clear, if unspoken, rules of reciprocity."[51] These good deeds were done simply to gain prestige and honor through acquiring positions of status in the city. One generous public doner even inscribed in stone on one of his buildings, a complaint about the lack of public recognition of his generosity.[52] While there was a cultural expectancy to reward generosity through rewarding them with public offices, Paul did not encourage this. All giving should be without strings attached.

The Episkopos

The descriptions of all the officers are very general and other Pauline books give no further information about their roles. It

---

just the Pastorals are considered. Payne, *Man and Woman*, 452.
49. Baugh, "Foreign World," 37–38.
50. Baugh, "Foreign World," 37–38.
51. Baugh, "Foreign World," 63
52. Baugh, "Foreign World," 63–64.

Women in Ministry

is difficult to draw specific conclusions about their roles or even what sex they were. Apart from Christ, there are never any names associated with the office of *episkopos* so there is no clear evidence that suggests an overseer cannot be a woman.[53] As Payne says, the Greek did not "have even one masculine pronoun or possessive, nor any other grammatical specification that Paul had men and not women in mind."[54]

The word *episkopos* (always in the singular), frequently translated overseer, means simply that, a person who is attentive to things or persons.[55] From its use in the Septuagint[56] and Josephus,[57] the "term implies general or specific oversight by political, religious, communal, military, or municipal individuals."[58] The qualifications describe a generally virtuous person who could just as easily be a pagan as a Christian, a female as well as a male. Onosander's example of a good general or Lucian's description of a good dancer reflects some of the same high moral standards.[59]

Ignatius' views on apostolic succession[60] can gain little support from the Pastoral Epistles as they deal primarily with who the *episkopos* is, rather than their role. An overseer has been described far less glamorously as the chief cook and bottle washer.[61] In a sense "he was the public face of the church"[62] and so was to be *anepilēmptos* (1 Tim 3:2–7), "one who has nothing which an

---

53. Payne, "Libertarian," 195.

54. Payne, "Libertarian," 196.

55. Mappes, "New Testament Elder," 164.

56. The word covers priestly oversight (Num 4:16), military leadership (Num 31:14), stewards (Jud 9:28), and also the superintendants of those who repaired the Temple (2 Chr 34:12, 17).

57. Josephus, *A.J.* 10:53; 12:254; 16:321.

58. Mappes, "New Testament Elder," 164–65.

59. Dibelius and Conzelmann, *Pastoral*, 160. Texts of pagan moral values are reproduced on pages 158–60.

60. Ignatius, *Magenesians* 6; *Trallians* 3. Fee believes that the New Testament itself functions as the apostolic succession. Fee, *1 and 2 Timothy*, 150.

61. Pietersen, *Polemic*, 104.

62. Pietersen, *Polemic*, 100.

The Ephesian Heresy and Ministry Roles

adversary could seize upon with which to base a charge."[63] Titus 1:7–9 uses the synonym *anenkletos*. Such a man could bear public examination. Their self-control in all areas of their life, including alcohol, would have been recognized by their society as classical Greek virtues[64] and as such would be seen as *kosmios* or "respectable." The emphasis on the need for exemplary behavior contrasts to that of the false teachers. Likewise, the call to moderation in the leaders stands against the aesthetic behavior of the heretics. The *episkopos* was to be reasonable in all his dealings, unlike the quarrelsome heretics. (Refer to Table 3)

False Teachers	Leaders
Some were persisting in sin 5:20	Must have a proven reputation for blameless behavior 5:22, 24, 25; 3:2, 4–7, 8, 10
Forbade marriage 4:3	Exemplary husbands and fathers 3:2, 4, 5, 12
Used "godliness" for financial gain 6:5	Not to be lovers of money 3:3, 8
Were quarrelsome and divisive 6:4–5	Are not to be quarrelsome but gentle 3:3

Table 3. Church leaders compared to the heretics in First Timothy

The qualifications for the *episkopos* were linked to the domestic setting. He was to be hospitable, a virtue commonly extolled (and so open to abuse) in early church literature.[65] Hospitality would have been very important "given the mobility and networking of those early communities, with their travelling apostles, prophets etc."[66] The ideal domestic scene is continued with the

---

63. Zodhiates, *Word Study Dictionary*, Ref 432.
64. Pietersen, *Polemic*, 100.
65. "Didache," 11–13; *1 Clem*, 10–12.
66. Pietersen, *Polemic*, 100.

episkopos being the husband of one wife and governing his family well and who in turn respect him. This also was recognized by the Greeks as a virtue.[67] As the head of the family had considerable power, so the *episkopos* would have also been seen as having real authority[68] over God's household.[69]

The function of the *episkopos* is most clearly seen in his role as *theou oikonomos* or "steward of God" (Titus 1:7). Slaves who functioned as business manager of the household were commonly called *oikonomos*.[70] Their owner's authority and power were entrusted to them, but this power was not the same, which was by right as a son's. Because it was delegated, the *episkopos* must have been chosen and was one who would have "set the moral tone of the community."[71] Again, also the imagery of the household is used and the *episkopos* is seen as one who keeps an eye on God's family.

Fulfilling the roll of *episkopos* was a good work and all were encouraged to aspire to this position (1 Tim 3:1 unlike James 3:1). The teaching role is important, but not stressed in First Timothy. The development of the exceptional life should have taken priority over the development of teaching skills as this life would have protected the teacher in his teaching and allowed the *episkopos* to stand before God without reproof at the judgment. Such character development was impossible in a new convert. The role of the *episkopos,* as a teacher is more important in Titus 1:6–9 but the crisis caused by those who were spreading false teachings also seems more pressing (Titus 1:10–13).

---

67. Isocretes, *Ad Nic.* 19.

68. The difference between secular and Christian authority is explored later in this chapter.

69. Pietersen, *Polemic,* 100.

70. This is based on the inscriptions on the tombs of slaves who have recorded their occupation. Pietersen, *Polemic,* 102.

71. Pietersen, *Polemic,* 103.

The Ephesian Heresy and Ministry Roles

The Presbyteroi

The *presbyteroi* (1 Tim 5:17) was the group that laid hands on Timothy (1 Tim 4:14), which points toward a formal group. The role of the different church officers would have been much simpler if it was not for Titus where *presbyteros* (1:5) is equated with *episkopos* (1:7) Further, in 1 Tim 3 there is no *presbyteroi*, referring only to the *episkopos* and the *diakonoi*. The term does appear in 1 Tim 5:1 where the context is simply an old man who is worthy of respect. This is similar to the way the word is used in Titus 2:2 where the elderly, just like the *episkopos*, should be setting a good example. *Presbyteroi* appears again in 1 Tim 5:17 where the good *presbyteroi* are worth double pay or honor for their ruling, preaching, and teaching.

This appears to be a definite role beyond simply being old men, but it is virtually impossible to determine what the relationship was between the *episkopos* and *presbyteroi* in the early Christian church. The term *presbyteroi* is used in the gospels for the elders of the Jewish people. Jerusalem, like the Greek cities, had been governed by a council of "elderly, experienced, and wise senior citizens called the *Gerousia*,[72] i.e., the Sanhedrin. This same group is referred to in Josephus as the *presbyteroi*. As the Christian community grew and developed a distinctly different identity, a possible role of the *presbyteroi* emerged, one of being a governing council.[73]

Because of their greater age, these men had more than just training. They had maturity and experience. Their ruling and teaching role would have allowed for the words *episkopos* and *presbyteroi* to be simple synonyms and the *episkopos* to be the leader of the *presbyteroi*. A suggestion put forward by Pietersen explains the role of the *presbyteroi*. These older members of the community were especially good as being bearers of the corporate memory and teachers of the tradition for which they received some financial

---

72. Pietersen, *Polemic*, 109.
73. Pietersen, *Polemic*, 110.

reward.[74] This suggests that their office is not at the same level as the *episkopos*, but Titus 1:7 works against this.

The Diakonoi

The qualifications for the *diakonoi* (deacon) were very similar to those of the *episkopos*. Again, the emphasis is not with what he (or she?) does, but what he (she?) is, i.e., his (or her?) moral qualities. While the *diakonoi* can be seen as fulfilling the roll of the servant within the household of God, it is an inadequate view to see him (or her?) just as a servant. Those who perform this role well would have had a very high standing in the community and their ministry built up their confidence in the faith (1 Tim 3:13). Paul was pleased to use this word as well as *dulos* (slave) to describe himself (Rom 1:1) and both words are used to describe Timothy (1 Tim 4:6; Phil 1:1).

The qualifications for the deacons are only marginally, if actually, inferior to those of the overseer and elder. There may be some blurring of the roles of elders and deacons. While eldership is a Spirit energized ministry with or without formal appointment,[75] it is also a function with set roles such as teaching. We know that some of the seven good men in Acts 6:3 whose official role was administering the charity of the church had powerful preaching and evangelistic skills. This was function without office.

Paul wrote, "Here is a trustworthy saying: Whoever aspires to be an overseer desires a noble task" (1 Tim 3:1 NASB). The qualifications for elders required that they be proven blameless and faithful in the Christian community, and this would have indicated "some level of prior ministry or function is required for eldership."[76] Paul's case in all offices was that competency in a lesser function was evidence of how the person would operate in the greater office. This function started in the management of

---

74. Pietersen, *Polemic*, 107.
75. Mappes, "New Testament Elder," 170.
76. Mappes, "New Testament Elder," 171.

their home and person and extended to the ministry of the church. As one writer says, "If one does not function effectively without office, how can he function effectively in office?"[77] In this manner, the office of deacon can be viewed as an apprenticeship for eldership where evidence of function can be seen. It is a place where the training for an exemplary life can begin. This blurring of roles becomes more important when we allow for female deacons.

The Widows

In the New Testament environment, women were dependent legally and financially, initially on their parents and then their husbands. Because of a shorter life span in New Testament times, the issue of widows was more acute as wives could become widows at a very early age. Charity toward widows has been a hallmark of both Judaism and Christianity (Jas 1:27). In the Pastoral Epistles, the duty toward them is recognized, but some, it appears, were expecting the church to take care of widows when in fact they themselves had a family responsibility to do just that (1 Tim 5:4). Financially the church should only have been concerned with those who needed genuine help and there was a responsibility on behalf of the widow to "receive it responsibly, setting an example of faith and piety."[78]

There was a list of enrolled widows (1 Tim 5:9) who were to receive the charity of the church, but only the elderly could be added to it. Young women were to be excluded as they would be distracted and remarry forsaking their commitment, which appears to be a vow of celibacy.[79] It was better for the young to remarry (1 Cor 7:9). There was a danger that the young women would be idle, visiting homes and spreading gossip (1 Tim 13–14). This visitation could also have been associated with spreading unorthodox teaching and keeping alive old wives' tales (1 Tim 4:7) as seen in

77. Mappes, "New Testament Elder," 171.

78. Pietersen, *Polemic*, 117.

79. The suggestion by Pietersen that this was a commitment to be espoused to Christ seems to go too far. Pietersen, *Polemic*, 119.

the *Acts of Paul*. These younger widows, through no fault of their own, would usually have had little if any formal education and, without their husbands, were devoid of any guidance. From the exclusions, some take the enrolled widows as a ministry order in the church with duties of prayer intercession and visitation. Others see this not as an order but as a list of those entitled to the charity of the church.[80]

The structure of 1 Tim 3 supports the idea that a social group, not an office, is in mind. The reference to the enrolled widows is not in the section dealing with the character of the office holders. The section addresses the older and younger women and finishes with the slaves. There is reference to presbyters here also, but they may not be "so much 'officers' as respected wise men of the community, who like the real widows, receive a 'pension' from the church."[81]

Nature of Teaching and Authority in the Early Church

Our image of teaching in a modern western church is of someone, usually a male, standing in front of a group of believers, explaining the meaning of a passage or verse or doctrine from an open Bible. Should there be a mistake there is usually other "teachers" on hand who are also biblically literate to correct any misrepresentation.[82] New Testament teaching was very different as it did not involve explaining texts in the modern sense. The Bible had not been completed and few would have had access to what was available. Likewise, catechisms with their structured learning had not yet been developed. The teachings of Jesus and the Apostles could only be shared in oral form. Just as the disciples rejected the testimony of the women about the resurrection, it would also have been dismissed by most men in all the places it was likewise proclaimed by a woman. Someone who was trusted to transmit the

---

80. Pietersen, *Polemic*, 117.
81. Pietersen, *Polemic*, 120.
82. Liefeld, "Plural," 150.

oral testimony accurately must have had a level of authority that it is difficult to appreciate now. Authority does not now come from the fallible memory of a teacher but from the written Word.[83]

Authority in the early church was not meant to be like that of secular leaders (Mark 10:35–45). It was not one of domination but of serving and protecting (Acts 20:25–31). Situations that sometimes exist in modern churches where pastors have considerable power is very far from the New Testament concept of authority where ministry is servanthood and being examples. Peter put this clearly, "Shepherd the flock of God among you, exercising oversight, not under compulsion but voluntarily, according to *the will of* God; and not with greed but with eagerness; **3** nor yet as domineering over those assigned to your care, but by proving to be examples to the flock" (1 Pet 5:2–3 NASB). Discussion on women in ministry often centers around what "authority" a woman should have. Instead of discussing what authority any person, male or female, should be permitted to have in a church where rank among believers is discouraged (Matt 18:1–4) it should concentrate on the ministry gift and how it can be used to serve. Ministry (or service) not the exercise of authority was meant to be and should still be the driver.[84]

Indirect Evidence of Women's Ministry

At no time does Paul deal comprehensively with women in ministry. Jennifer Stiefel claims most evidence for woman's ministry is indirect and gives the example of Pliny torturing two female slaves and noting that they were *ministrae* (possibly *diakonos*).[85] On one hand, Paul is only recorded as travelling with men[86] and it is clear that the main burden of founding the Christian church

---

83. Liefeld, "Plural," 151.
84. Liefeld, "Plural," 147.
85. Pliny, *Ep.* 10.96.
86. The claim that this follows the pattern established by Jesus is a leap too far, e.g., Duinkerken, "Women," 344. Jesus did at times travel with women (Luke 8:1–3), which would have been radical for a rabbi.

lay with men.[87] On the other, if it wasn't for the greetings in the final chapter of Romans we could miss how thoroughly integrated women were into the lives of the churches he established. Their involvement was far from being inconsequential! Two thirds of Paul's references to women are found in that chapter, which shines a light on the possibilities of women for ministry.

Romans commends Phoebe, the female deacon from Cenchreae (just outside Corinth), to the Roman church. There is no female form of deacon in the New Testament.[88] The word is frequently translated as "servant," avoiding the perception that she may have had a leadership role. This is despite using "minister" or "deacon" in other occurrences of the word for men, especially when *diakonos* implies official ruling.[89] Unfortunately, when Paul mentioned a ministry role or work for the gospel against a female name, he did not attach a job description and we are left wondering what their precise duties were. Douglas Moo argues strongly that we cannot be sure that Phoebe was a fully fledged deacon, probably a helper or protector but also possibly an administrator of charitable work.[90] But this latter role in Acts was a male prerogative (Acts 6:1–6) so even if he is right there is at minimum a significant shift toward women. Even Moo, a critic of women teaching, admits that there is no doubt that Phoebe was some sort of minister at Cenchreae.[91] As the trusted bearer of the letter, it is not unreasonable to suggest she may have been called on to interpret sections of the letter if they were not clear.[92] Her role shows that the requirement for a deacon being a one woman man (1 Tim 3:12) was not a hard and fast rule.

---

87. Duinkerken, "Women," 327. He calculates that 82 percent of the people mentioned in his letters as being involved with him in mission were men and 18 percent were women.

88. Payne, "Libertarian," 194.

89. Payne, "Libertarian," 196. Refer also Rengstorf, "διδάσκω," 2.135–65.

90. Moo, "Interpretation," 210.

91. Moo, "Interpretation," 210.

92. Keener, *Paul*, 238.

The Ephesian Heresy and Ministry Roles

Phoebe is also described as a *prostatis*, a feminine form of a word, which in First Timothy has the sense of both "leading" and "caring for" which "agrees with the distinctive nature of the office in the NT."[93] Had this person been male they would have been seen as having a very senior leadership role. The different ways the words used of Phoebe are "toned down"[94] compared to when they are used of men opens translators to the accusation of sexual prejudice

Further, it is entirely possible that the Book of Romans is actually a copy that was sent to Ephesus[95] which, if correct, suggests that, in churches Paul founded and/or organized, women had leadership roles. Paul even referred to Junia, a common Roman female name,[96] who was outstanding among the apostles.[97] Those that suppose Junia was not a female apostle do so on the assumption that women cannot be apostles, not on the text.[98] As her name was used in conjunction with a male travelling companion, Andronicus, propriety would demand that they be either brother and sister or a husband-and-wife team. We also know of Euodia and Syntyche who struggled beside Paul as fellow workers (*syzygos*) alongside Clement in the work of the gospel (Phil 4:2–3). Their personal dispute troubled Paul lest their work for the gospel be diverted. It begs the question of whether the traditional interpretation of Paul's teaching was in contradiction with his practice. He

---

93. Reicke, "προστῆναι," 702–703.

94. Mickelson, "Egalitarian," 190.

95. Koester, "Ephesos," 123.

96. Payne, "Libertarian," 184. There is little evidence for Junia being a contraction of the masculine Junianus. Keener, *Paul*, 242. Duinkerken states that Junia is found in more than 250 inscriptions in Rome and in each case, it is female and that a male form of the word is completely unknown. Duinkerken, "Women," 336.

97. Moo is probably correct that she is a small "a" apostle as opposed to a capital "A" Apostle who has seen Christ. Moo, "Interpretation," 209. But she is a messenger nonetheless with an authority apparently exceeding that of an overseer.

98. Keener, *Paul*, 242. Payne argues that the only textual variant is to an even more common female name. Payne, *Man and Woman*, 66

had instructed the Corinthian church to be subject to and recognize every coworker (1 Cor 16:16, 18).

Paul was so comfortable with his friends Priscilla and Aquilla that he was in secular business with and shared ministry with them. Priscilla is mentioned three times before Aquila, which was very uncommon. She must have had a strong personality and demonstrated great ability for this to occur as Paul calls her his fellow worker in Christ Jesus (Rom 16:3–5). Priscilla and her husband taught[99] Apollos, a man and a teacher of men, and Acts records this without any unfavorable comment. If the teaching role of Priscilla was incorrect, then Paul was open to the charge of hypocrisy. The two missionary teams, Junia and Andronicus, and Priscilla and Aquila, still allow for the traditional understanding of male headship and the woman acting under his authority.[100] We cannot assert that these women had an authoritative leadership role in the church outside of their husband's (or brother's?) authority. Where we are not directed is how is their ministry changed should the husband die. Are they relegated to the back room and the kitchen, or only allowed to teach women and children or even some other tasks well below their abilities and calling a few days prior? And heaven forbid that the husband should die on one of their travels.

---

99. Moo's argument seems weak when he maintains Priscilla did not *teach* anyone, she merely *instructed* Apollos. Moo, "Interpretation," 202. He understands teaching as "involving the careful transmission of Christian tradition and the authoritative proclamation of God's will based on that tradition and study of scriptures," which is generally the contemporary understanding. Moo, "Interpretation," 207. He claims that the word "teach" is narrower than our present usage but does not define it. Moo, "Interpretation," 202. This is not helpful when the word is applied widely in a contemporary setting to restrict women's ministry. Hughes, who takes a similar viewpoint on women's ministry, says it was "teaching." Hughes, "Living Out," 108.

100. We know that the apostles travelled with their wives and Paul claims the same right for himself and his assistants (1 Cor 9:5). Clement of Alexandria (c. 150–c. 215) said, "It was through them that the Lord's teaching penetrated also the women's quarters without any scandal being aroused." Clement of Alexandria, *Strometeis*, 3.6.53. His statement is generations after the event and is mixed with his view of celibacy, claiming they travelled in a brother and sister relationship. That same passage does affirm female deacons.

The Ephesian Heresy and Ministry Roles

The New Testament church was "built on the foundation of the apostles and prophets" (Eph 2:20, NASB). Philip's four daughters were all prophets (Acts 21:9 see also Anna in Luke 2:26–38 and "daughters" in Acts 2:17.) Paul assumed that women would be prophesying in the assembly in Corinth (1 Cor 11:5). Any attempt to see the prophet's role as inferior to that of the teacher are put aside by Eph 3:5. Paul, in speaking of the universal gospel says, "The mystery of Christ, which in other generations was not made known to mankind, as it has now been revealed to His holy apostles and prophets in the Spirit (NASB)." In 1 Cor 12:28, teaching is ranked after the prophets. (See also Acts 13:1.) It is difficult to assert that New Testament prophecy was not authoritative. It would be wrong to set the Spirit-led ministries against the official roles in the New Testament church. Prophesy could be mixed with error and needed discernment, but so could Christian teaching and it likewise needed to be received with as much discernment and still does. Both had to be weighed against Apostolic message. When New Testament prophecy is accepted as authoritative it becomes a powerful argument against limiting the teaching role of women.[101] Through this gift the Spirit himself affirms their dignity and authority. If women were more susceptible to error because of their gender, why were they permitted to prophesy in the first place.

The New Testament uses terms describing the activities of some women that were normally associated with leadership positions: "explaining the way of God more accurately" (Acts 18:26), "deacon" (Rom 16:1), "ruler" (Rom 16:2), "my fellow worker in Christ Jesus" (Rom 16:3; Phil 4:3), "apostle" (Rom 16:7), "worked hard in the Lord" (Rom 16:6, 12), and "contended at my side in the cause of the gospel" (Phil 4:3). It is reasonable to argue that "if women are represented in the New Testament as fulfilling functions known to be associated with leadership positions, it is reasonable to assume that they were in fact appointed to the offices associated with such activities."[102] The term Paul used for "worked" described

---

101. Schreiner, "Interpretation," 193.
102. Payne, "Libertarian," 197.

his own manual labors so he could preach the gospel for free (1 Cor 15:10) but also "the missionary and pastoral work of others."[103]

The indirect evidence strongly suggests that women took a leadership role in the church, at least at the level of deacon and their functional role may well have been greater than their office. Their function, if not their office, allowed them to work hard in the Lord and win the respect of the Apostle (Rom 16:1–3, 6, 12, 13, 15). In the case of Priscilla, she fulfilled the role of an *episkopos*. Any ban on women in leadership seems to be related to the circumstances in Ephesus than a blanket authoritative statement. In the same time frame, "Phoebe had been praised in her position of authority while the women at Ephesus had been restrained."[104]

If Paul was completely opposed to women's ministry, it is hard to explain the appearance and acceptance of *The Acts of Paul and Thecla*.[105] In this early Christian "novel," Paul commissioned Thecla to preach, teach, and baptize as a woman missionary. The Pastoral Epistles, along with the indirect evidence, show that the role for women was generally advanced for its time, but not especially advanced for Ephesus. Women in Asia Minor were more conspicuous in religious life than elsewhere.[106] This prominent role would not have been unnoticed by Ephesian Jews and Christians.

Direct Evidence of Women's Ministry

It is possible, however, that there was an expectation of women *diakonoi* in 1 Tim 3:11. This passage deals with the qualifications of deacons (vv. 8–13), but also refers to women having the same qualifications applying to them. They were to be serious or worthy of honor, at a time when not a great deal of honor was given to women. The same adjective *semnous* is used of men in 1 Tim 3:8. Also they are not to be slanderers, which is the charge levelled

---

103. Hauck, "κόπος, κοπιάω," 3.827

104. Spencer, "Eve at Ephesus," 221.

105. Part of the apocryphal *Acts of Paul,* possibly written sometime between 100–160. The remainder of the book is only known through fragments.

106. Strelan, *Paul,* 120.

The Ephesian Heresy and Ministry Roles

against the older women in 2 Tim 3:2–3. As with the charge to the male *diakonoi* to hold fast to the mystery of the faith (1 Tim 3:9) these women were to be faithful or trustworthy in everything. While this may have referred only to the wives of the *diakonoi*, the sense of the passage suggests not. The qualities were not gender specific and in no way differentiated from those of the men. More compellingly, Paul refers to Phoebe as a *diakonos* (Rom 16:1). Had Paul not mentioned Phoebe's name and role, there would not be any evidence of an actual woman serving in this role usually considered the task of men.

The word "likewise" reflects 1 Tim 3:8, where it signals the beginning of a new topic. Here we would be expecting to encounter a new group that related to the overseers and deacons. The plural noun for woman has no definite article. Three ways "likewise" can be interpreted are:

- Possibly it is an anarthrous noun[107] used as general reference to all women but this means that the high requirements for just some men were imposed on all women.[108] This is unreasonable.

- Alternatively, terms of relationship when spoken of in general do not need the article.[109] This would make the women in a relationship with the male deacons, i.e., their wives. This is the traditional view but working against this is that there are no requirements for the wife of the *episkopos*

- A third possibility is again that it is an anarthrous noun to specify a counterpart with the "appropriate occupational term implied, but unexpressed, that is intending something like 'women' (ones) likewise."[110] This is said to be the more widely accepted understanding.[111]

---

107. A noun without an article.
108. Stiefel, "Women," 445.
109. Stiefel, "Women," 446.
110. Stiefel, "Women," 447.
111. Stiefel, "Women," 453.

Women in Ministry

What was the role of these women? Roles for women *diakonoi* as suggested by Loyd Pietersen were that they waited on tables and assisted at the baptism of women.[112] These menial roles seem inadequate for people with such high morals and character. They did not have a separate name to the male *diakonoi* and this may well be because they were not a separate group, but were included among the *diakonoi*.

Though they may have prophesied, neither the male nor the female *diakonos* are seen as teachers, which was the role of the *episkopos*. The Pastoral Epistles (1 Tim 2:9–12) and First Corinthians (14:34–35) do show reservations about women teaching men. While the verses are similar, the settings are very different. Paul had problems with particular women in particular churches. In Corinth, the women, along with those who spoke in tongues and the prophets, were disrupting the meetings. In the Pastoral Epistles, the emphasis is on peace and quiet while learning[113] opposed to the disruption of the heretics. The word *manthano* (1 Tim 2:11) implies structured leaning. While this indicates that the women were recent converts, we must weigh the fact that the women were being instructed at all! Female God-fearers as well as Jews were excluded from instruction in the scriptures in the synagogues.[114] The women in Ephesus had already submitted themselves to the false teachers and, unknowingly, even to Satan (1 Tim 1:3–7; 4:1). Instead, these women should have submitted to those who teach the words of faith (1 Tim 4:6). Rather than never teach, they were to learn properly.[115] Learning[116] in silence was not an imposition on women who had been too vocal in spreading false teaching but an invitation to learn as the men did. It contrasts the deception of Eve in verse fourteen. Simon, the son of Gamaliel, Paul's teacher,

---

112. Pietersen, *Polemic*, 114.
113. Padgett, "Wealthy," 24.
114. Padgett, "Wealthy," 24.
115. Payne, "Liberterian," 178.
116. "If [women's] susceptibility to deception was that severe we would have expected Paul to bar them from being taught as was apparently the common practice in synagogues at that time. Payne, "Liberterian," 178.

said, "All my days I grew up among the sages, and I have found nothing better for a person than silence. Study is not the most important thing, but deed: whosoever indulges in too many words brings about sin."[117]

Though Gamaliel's zealous student Paul moved to a position contrary to Jewish practice at the time (though seemingly in keeping with his teacher Gamaliel),[118] there was really nothing new in this. During the exodus and conquest, women, not just men, were urged to attend the reading of the Law (Deut 31:12; Josh 8:35). Sadly though, by the first century women were exempted from learning the law so they could concentrate on being homemakers.[119] The best a woman could hope for would be to hear (as opposed to learning) from the back lobby and have no part of the synagogue service. With Mary and Martha, Jesus had encouraged such learning taking precedence over household duties (Luke 10:38–42).

---

117. Mishna, *Pirkei Avot*. 1.17
118. Payne, *Man and Woman*, 35–38.
119. Spencer, "Eve at Ephesus," 218.

3

Exposition of First Timothy 2:8–15

Having discussed women in ministry as a general principal in the previous chapter, the apparent contradictory statements about their role in 1 Tim 2:8–15 must be carefully scrutinized because the passage is not as straightforward as some of our translations seem to indicate. Anne Bowman, a supporter of women in ministry, stated the problem clearly, saying we are confronted with a difficult passage that contains:

- Unusual vocabulary (*authenteó*, *hésuchia*);
- Awkward grammar (the link between verses 14 and 15);
- References to the Old Testament (Gen 2–3) whose usage in 1 Tim 2:13–14 needs to be determined;
- Significant theological issues, e.g., the use of *sózó*; and
- A flow of thought that is not so clear as it first appears.[1]

Despite this textual uncertainty and a poorly understood church situation, we find not just rank and file believers but also scholars fluent in Greek making varied yet still dogmatic

---

1. Bowman, "Women in Ministry," 194.

Exposition of First Timothy 2:8–15

statements with enormous consequences for church practice. I am not making the mistake of being equally dogmatic that the following interpretation is correct. My interpretation says no more than a passage normally taken to exclude women's ministry can also legitimately be used to support one that is inclusive.

But before we even start to see what these verses say about a woman's role in a public Christian meeting, can these verses be struck out altogether? Paul started chapter 2 looking at how and why a Christian should interact with the governmental needs of society, but it has been argued the following verses, eight to fifteen, are not concerned with public worship as such but are more directed toward the home. With chapter 3 dealing with church offices, this would mean that Paul was giving rounded advice on the three main spheres of Christian living. There is a striking parallel between our passage and 1 Pet 3:1–7 where Peter is clearly talking about husband-and-wife relationships. The comparisons with First Peter are so impressive that Dibelius and Conzelmann express surprise that our passage is placed in a section dealing with public worship and see it supporting their view that the regulations of First Timothy "represent a collection of various materials."[2] Similarities include reference to the prayer life of husbands, modest clothing, wearing gold, braided hair, quietness, and even a wife not vaunting over her (unbelieving) husband with her superior knowledge.[3]

A common source has been suggested that would point us toward seeing this passage in First Timothy as also household related.[4] The terms *anēr* and *gynē* that are seen in verses 7–15 and that are normally translated "man"/"men" and "women"/"women" can just as easily be translated "husband"/"husbands" and "wife"/"wives."[5] If this understanding is correct, the "similarity of these passages goes beyond the concern for wifely submission to include a shared warning to husbands against domestic strife that

---

2. Dibelius and Conzelmann, *Pastoral*, 5
3. Hugenberger, "Women," 352, 356 358
4. Hugenberger, "Women," 355.
5. Hugenberger, "Women," 351.

would undermine their prayer life."[6] It should be remembered that our strict western delineation between home and the public worship service in a separate building did not exist then. Services were held in their own private home or that of another believer. Why would a devout believer act differently in their private household than when serving in God's household?[7]

If Paul was referring to wives, not women in general, any restriction he would make in verses 8–15 relate only to a wife teaching and having authority over her husband and not necessarily applying to a public setting. It is "a man" singular, not "men" plural, that she is not to have authority over. However, there are also important differences, e.g., Peter refers to unbelieving husbands and it is clarified that Peter has wives in view, not women in general. Further working against this being only a husband/wife setting is that Paul would be equally concerned about the adornment of single women. The words "every place," "prayer," and "teaching" make public worship more likely.[8] Perhaps the most we can say is that it is tantalizing but ultimately adds nothing positive to our understanding of a woman's role in a worship service where the authority could be very different.[9] Here a man's slave could be, theoretically at least, his elder[10] and historically we do know that female slaves served as deacons.

> **8** *Therefore I want the men everywhere to pray, lifting up holy hands without anger or disputing.* (NASB)

Verse 8. The passage in the second half of chapter 2, which deals with peace and stability in the church, starts with "therefore," so what follows in these final verses is built firmly on the previous seven verses. There are similar thoughts recuring in the

---

6. Hugenberger, "Women," 356
7. Spencer, "Leadership," 5.
8. Schreiner, "Interpretation," 179.
9. Hugenberger, "Women," 351.
10. F. F. Bruce states that there "is sufficient evidence that this was not merely a theoretical possibility. Bruce, *Galatians*, 189. There is a tradition that the freed slave Onesimus became the Bishop of Ephesus.

Exposition of First Timothy 2:8–15

second half of the chapter, peace (2:2), authority (2:2), salvation (2:4), and coming to a knowledge of the truth (2:4). Paul opened his letter to Timothy with clear purpose, which was to stop people who were hindering God's work through false teachings. For all their lofty appearance, they were propounding meaningless trivia (1:14–17) and distracted their hearers from the enormity of the salvation found in Christ (1:12–16). He then opens chapter 2 with first things first (2:1) and progresses to instruct his emissary on how the church should set about finding peace. His instructions are directed to those groups that needed them most, men who had anger and were disputing and women who were involved with spreading false teaching. That is not to say there was not an overlap or mutual application.

Paul has called upon his apostolic authority in verse seven so his opening words about public prayer "I want" are to be taken seriously, not as wishful thinking. He believes that what is of primary importance is that there is peace and stability in both society and the church so that the gospel is promoted without any hindrance. Peace in society is meant to come through prayer for salvation that crosses the boundaries of race, creed, social status, and authority (and presumably sexes.) Notably, hands that in some cases were once objects of fear when raised in anger in a domestic setting are now to be raised in prayer as a source of blessing and peace. This was the apostle's own experience as a blasphemer, persecutor, and a violent man (1 Tim 1:13).

The roles of men and women (or husband and wife to maintain the household model)[11] in public worship are contrasted. These different roles have been taken to justify an inferior ministry role for women who could rule in their own family (1 Tim 5:14) but not in God's family.[12] Men prepared their hearts to pray in a worthy manner while women (already commanded to pray in verse one) attended to deportment, good works and learning quietly. William Hendriksen describes this lesser role, "The presence of women in the religious assembly is of course assumed. Paul's point is that these

11. Dunn, "First," 801.
12. Gealy, "First," 403.

women should pray as Hannah did. She prayed in her heart, only her lips moved, but her voice was not heard"[13] (1 Sam 1:13). Some would also see these verses as an attempt by the "author" to rid the church of feminist practices that had crept in by restoring the traditional synagogue practice of males leading prayers.[14] But this passage can equally be translated in the following manner. "As far as prayer is concerned, I wish . . . that men everywhere would raise up holy hands without thought of anger or strife and the women do likewise in modest deportment."[15] Even if difference in roles between male and female can be established, woman's spiritual inferiority does not follow (Gal 3:28). When addressing the Corinthians, Paul had already accepted their right to pray (1 Cor 11:5).

Raising ritually cleansed hands during prayer was a common practice[16] but it was the heart rather than the physical act that is viewed by God. Holy hands stemmed from a cleansed conscience and a demeanor "without anger or argument."[17] Interpersonal conflicts should have gone. That, rather than physical actions, gave evidence that the argumentative spirit of the heretics had been avoided. There was no difference between men and women in this. Very importantly, it was all men who were to pray in verse eight, which went against the Jewish priestly system seen at the Jerusalem temple (and the pagan temples?) though the synagogue had been open to men to pray.[18]

> **9** *I also want the women to dress modestly, with decency and propriety, adorning themselves, not with elaborate hairstyles or gold or pearls or expensive clothes,* **10** *but with good deeds, appropriate for women who profess to worship God.* (NASB)

13. Hendriksen, *1&2 Thessalonians*, 103.
14. Gealy, "First," 403.
15. Dibelius and Conzelmann, *Pastoral*, 44.
16. Jewish ritual purification is probably in mind but the expression in the Greek tragedies also carries this meaning. Dibelius and Conzelmann, *Pastoral*, 44.
17. Dibelius and Conzelmann, *Pastoral*, 44.
18. Bray, *Pastoral*, 164.

Verses 9–10. There was nothing new or unreasonable to call the Ephesian women to a life of modesty and humility as these very characteristics were praised in the priestesses in the pagan religions who still had a very public presence.[19] What is new is the opportunity for women to interact with men with whom they are not related so there were few social customs to guide acceptable behavior. How they used their freedoms in this setting would have a big impact on how the church was perceived.[20] There is a need to balance freedoms and responsibilities. What is refreshing is that Paul addresses women (and children and slaves) directly. Often the Greco-Roman moralists would speak to them through their husbands.[21] Paul gives them credit for knowing that their appearance and actions are important to God. As well, the exercise of good deeds, along with the discipleship of younger women meant that they were no longer totally cloistered at home.

Fred Gealy claims that the author considered that a woman who wants to pray in church is capable of almost any lewdness![22] Greek hairstyles were normally simple, being parted in the middle and pinned at the back or held in place with a scarf or band.[23] The elaborate hairstyle that Paul refers to was a relatively new trend and Baugh dates its beginning to about ten years prior to his visit to Ephesus.[24] To prepare hair the way Paul describes took a lot of leisure time and wealth and was probably done by a trained slave.[25] This Roman style was promoted through statues of the empresses and some coins minted in the city and carried with it "connotations of imperial luxury and the infamous licentiousness of women like Messalina and Poppaea."[26] It is uncertain what is intended. Was it braiding that was forbidden or what was braided into the

19. Baugh, "Foreign World," 46–47, 62.
20. Bray, *Pastoral*, 167.
21. Baugh, "Foreign World," 44.
22. Gealy, "First," 405.
23. Baugh, "Foreign World," 54.
24. Baugh, "Foreign World," 56.
25. Baugh, "Foreign World," 54.
26. Baugh, "Foreign World," 55–56.

hair?[27] Pliny's example states the extreme of this extravagance, "I have seen Lollia Paulina [wife of Emperor Caligula] covered with emeralds and pearls gleaming all over her head, hair, ears, neck, and fingers, to the value of a million dollars."[28] Such immodesty would have precluded any woman from teaching.[29] It should be noted that some who advocate for the total ban on women teaching men would see the prohibition of women wearing gold and pearls as excessive literalism.[30]

The Christian woman should not be hoarding and displaying her possessions but should be generous to God's people. She should be adorned by her godly attitude that shows itself in good works.[31] The outward element of their modest attire speaks to the preparation of their hearts. The author is not saying that women's clothing was to be unfashionable or tasteless. Neither does it mean that women deliberately be dressed in a manner below their status and so equally bring attention to themselves. Good works, evidenced through careful choice of attire, are introduced as evidence of true faith (similarly Eph 2:10; Heb 10:24) but in the acknowledged Pauline epistles works are normally regarded as the opposite of faith (e.g., Rom 3:27–28).

The reference to "everywhere" in verse eight should not be limited to public worship as prayer and modest attire apply equally to the home as with childbearing and indeed the whole of life where good deeds are to be seen by outsiders. Some limit the application of these verses to the worship services[32] but it must be

---

27. Hoag, *Wealth*, 68. Hoag further points out that the description of Anthia representing Artemis in the Ephesian Tale has her having braided hair and that first-century statues of her have a similar braided style. Xenophon, *Ephesiaca*, 1.2.6, Hoag, *Wealth*, 75

28. Pliny the Elder, *Nat.* 9.58.

29. Payne suggests that this immodesty may be linked back to the way the prostitutes at the temple of Artemis ministered. Payne, "Libertarian," 192. The evidence is against such prostitution actually being carried on.

30. Schreiner, "Interpretation," 181.

31. This was a quality also valued by the female followers of Artemis. Brough, "Apostle," 164.

32. Bowman, "Women in Ministry," 203.

asked whether these verses are actually referring only to that time? There were probably numerous home churches and "every place" of 1 Tim 2:8 may have referred to each place where believers were gathered.[33] But the references to prayer in 2:1 and 2:8 should not be taken to mean that prayer was a practice primarily intended for public worship. These virtues would have first been mastered in the home.

> 11 *A woman should learn in quietness and full submission.*
> 12 *I do not permit a woman to teach or to assume authority over a man; she must be quiet.* (NASB)

Verses 11 and 12. We have come from two culturally conditioned commands, praying with raised hands and not wearing braided hair to a prohibition on women teaching, which the traditional understanding takes as universal in all ages. We have also come from Paul providing negative commands to correct poor behaviors to the prohibition of another ungodly behavior but teaching is generally regarded as good behavior.[34] Were women to be excluded from teaching because they were uneducated? Greek education of boys had as its primary focus empowering pupils to be good public speakers and the first skills acquired were memory and breathing control. The central skill for statesmanship was being able to deliver a persuasive argument (rhetoric) through public speaking (oratory).[35] These are useful skills for a teacher and no woman from Ephesus is recorded with this skill, but Paul did not require this as a qualification for teachers or elders and even admits that he is not a good speaker (2 Cor 11:6).

This does not mean that all women were uneducated, it just happened privately and was necessary to some degree in the upper classes as they may have to run a large household.[36] However, poorly educated women were likely to be heavily involved in the heresy, a problem that appears to be unique to the Ephesian

---

33. Fee, *1 and 2 Timothy*, 145.
34. Hübner, "Revisiting αὐθεντέω," 68.
35. Baugh, "Foreign World," 57.
36. Baugh, "Foreign World," 59.

church. Considering this, "Paul provided a short-range solution: 'Do not teach' (under the present circumstances); and a long-range solution: 'Let them learn.'"[37] This, as has been shown, was a liberating, not restrictive command in Ephesus. The emphasis is on the way they learned. It was similarly recommended that men be silent in 2 Thess 3:12 (quietness, RSV), which does not imply a total ban on speaking. To *have authority* is a natural partner for receiving in quietness.[38]

These two verses are directed to women generally, not wives specifically. The instructions about men and prayer and women and adornment were directed to a worshiping community, not a family. It appears that it was normal for women to pray and prophesy in a worship service (1 Cor 11:5) and further, to come with a psalm, a teaching, a revelation, a tongue, or an interpretation (1 Cor 14:26). Paul is either contradicting himself or we are reading too much into this verse. This active female role, even if it did break social boundaries, was edifying and met with God's approval. Therefore, *quietness* is probably a better translation than silence.[39] If "structural subordination"[40] is intended, it would describe the situation of a woman who has to learn the Christian message correctly from a true teacher of the faith. It may also be referring to the practice of listening to lectures in silence, a requirement of men also.[41] It says nothing of what happens when she has learned all the teacher has to offer. Whatever is meant here, it must not be in conflict with divinely sanctioned examples such as those of Deborah and Huldah.[42] Nor should it be in conflict with

37. Keener, "Was Paul For," para. 25

38. Payne, "Libertarian," 176; Moo, "Interpretation," 203.

39. The meaning ranges from silence (Acts 22:2) to rest and quietness (1 Tim 2:2; 2 Thess 3:12). Bowman, "Women in Ministry," 199; Payne, "Libertarian," 170. Moo disagrees claiming this is the only word in Paul's vocabulary which clearly means silence. Moo, "Interpretation," 200. He agrees the word means quietness in 2 Thess 3:12. But the argument ultimately seems circular; because as women are not to teach men the meaning must be "silence."

40. Johnson, *First and Second*, 201

41. Huizenga, *1–2 Timothy*; 1 Tim 2:25.

42. Harris, "Why Did Paul," 348. There are seven prophetesses recognized

Exposition of First Timothy 2:8–15

verses such as "The Lord announces the word, and the women who proclaim it are a mighty throng" (Ps 68:11 NASB). Unless, of course, there is less grace in the new covenant than the old.

Silence does not indicate submission, which could have been a detriment to learning.[43] The teachable quiet nature Paul urges upon the Ephesian women was the opposite of the heretics. Should this be any different for men? But who should the women be "submissive" to? There are four possibilities:

- Her husband,
- The church elder,
- Sound doctrine, or even
- Contemporary culture.[44]

The first option is unlikely as the focus was on male and female worshipers as a group. The second is favored in the commentaries by Kent[45] and Lock.[46] It is most likely that the third option or a combination of options two and three is meant, i.e., the women were to submit themselves only to those elders that taught sound doctrine.[47] Should this be any different for men? But this submission of a wife to her husband must be balanced by the command, also by Paul, that submission in a marriage is not a one-way street but is mutual (Eph 5:21–34). Any submission by a wife was seen as coming with a greater responsibility from the husband toward his wife by loving his wife totally and sacrificially.

Some see Paul's personal view[48] in the words *epitrepō*, "I do not permit,"[49] and it begs the question of who did permit it!

---

in Judaism: Sarah, Miriam, Deborah, Hannah, Abigail, Huldah, and Esther.

43. Payne, "Libertarian," 171.

44. Padgett, "Wealthy Women," 20. His argument is that in an environment of persecution, the church should be acting with caution.

45. Kent, *Pastoral*, 114.

46. Lock, *Pastoral*, 32.

47. Bowman, "Women in Ministry," 200

48. Bowman, "Women in Ministry," 200 n.18.

49. Payne argues that that in the LXX and the New Testament that the

A similar verse (1 Cor 14:34), where Paul says, "I do not permit" goes on to say (14:37) that it is the Lord's commandment, so it is unlikely this is just an opinion. Paul could have written, "I will never permit . . ." using the future tense, as is done in Matt 26:33, "I will never be offended," or he could have used the subjunctive,[50] as occurs twice in Heb 13:5, "I will never leave you nor forsake you." A formulation similar to either of these verses would have indicated a continuing prohibition, but Paul gave no indication that verse 12 should be understood as a continuing prohibition."[51] Moo, who disagrees with women teaching men, agrees that the verb is used fourteen out of eighteen times for "temporarily limited situations."[52] He then cites Rom 12:1 to support a continuing ban.[53] "I am beseeching you, brothers, to offer your bodies as living sacrifices." There seems a big gulf between accepting a call to holiness as universal, and accepting what could be a repressive social situation as a divinely inspired norm.

The difficulty in declaring *epitrepō* as a universal prohibition can be seen in Matt 19:8–9 and Mark 10:4, where the term is used of Moses "permitting" divorce and Jesus teaching contrary to it. Schreiner, a scholar who is strident in rejecting women teaching men in public, says, "The context, not the term 'permitted,' determines the universal or temporary prohibition."[54] He goes on to say there is nothing in the verse to indicate whether we are dealing with a universal or a temporary measure and it only achieves meaning from the next verse where Eve had the misfortune to be formed after Adam.

---

expression "I am not permitting" is never used of a continuing prohibition. Payne, "Libertarian," 191. He has a valid argument when he points out that the restrictions in the immediate context (attire and gestures when praying) are not considered universal. Payne, "Libertarian," 191.

50. The subjunctive mood is the verb form used to explore a hypothetical situation or to express a wish, a demand, or a suggestion.

51. Payne, "Libertarian," 172.

52. Moo, "Interpretation," 200–201.

53. Moo, "Interpretation," 200–201.

54. Schreiner, "Interpretation," 190.

Exposition of First Timothy 2:8-15

The Old Testament teaching ministry, which was carried through into the New Testament, involved knowledge and skills but its final goal was the person's will with the intention of promoting the achievement of God's will.[55] There are many words that could be used for teaching but the one used here is *didaskō*. In the biblical setting, *didaskō* had a far wider goal than secular Greek where its use was intellectual and authoritative and there was little religious use.[56] The word carries a good connotation when it is used of John the Baptist (Luke 3:12), Nicodemus (John 3:10), the scribes (Luke 2:46), Paul (1 Tim 2:7), Timothy (1 Tim 4:11), and overseers (1 Tim 3:2). Surprisingly it is not used of the apostles. It is also used in a bad sense of the false teachers and in a general way in that nature teaches that long hair is a disgrace in a man (1 Cor 11:14–15). Because it is such a general term and covers matters that Paul elsewhere approves for women it is reasonably argued that there should be qualifications to its use in this verse.[57]

The gift of teaching has been described as "the spiritual gift of teaching [which] enables individuals to grasp revelation that already has been given and to communicate this truth effectively to others."[58] It is precisely this giftedness that complicates the issue. If the Spirit has given a gift, there must be a legitimate means for its use. It is not that women are necessarily bad teachers; Timothy was taught accurately by his grandmother Lois and mother Eunice, and Apollos was instructed equally well by Priscilla. Importantly, Paul saw no difference in the depth and sincerity of faith between these women and Timothy (2 Tim 1:5), his trusted emissary to Ephesus. Lois and Eunice made such an impact on him that Paul urged Timothy to contemplate just who he had learned the saving truths of the Scriptures from (2 Tim 3:14–15). The question is whether women can say the same things publicly in an official capacity that they say privately!

---

55. Saucy, "Women's Prohibition," 83.
56. Rengstorf, *Didasko*, 141.
57. Payne, *Man and Woman*, 328–34.
58. Bowman, "Women in Ministry," 201.

What is the relationship in these verses between *teaching* and *authority*? They are joined with *oude*, which "joins closely interrelated concepts that reinforce each other or express a single coherent idea."[59] Examples exist (2 Cor 7:12; 2 Thess 3:7–8) where *oude* joins concepts where one is positive and the other negative. Teaching and whatever *authenteō* implies (positive or negative) are not two separate prohibitions but something more focused that involves the two. Paul could have easily clarified the situation by saying that he does not permit a woman to be an elder, but he chose not to and used verbs not nouns. The implication is that he was thinking of an action, not an office.[60]

The word translated by the NASB as "assume authority over," *authenteō*, is said to be a colloquial term,[61] which makes it rare in Greek literature. Al Wolters maintains that, up to 312 AD, the word is only found eight times and most of these are debatable due to a dubious text, unclear context or uncertain dating.[62] This makes it impossible to decide what nuance Paul had in mind when he chose that word rather than *exousía* ("authority") and *exousiázō* ("to have authority").[63] The word moved from being a rarely recorded general word to becoming a technical term in church circles which can result in reading back into the text a later meaning it did not initially have.[64] Much of our understanding of this verse will hinge on whether this word is seen negatively, e.g., "usurp authority" as in the Authorised Version, or positively, e.g., "have authority" as used by the English Standard Version. While most English versions translate this word positively, not all do with one

---

59. Hugenberger, "Women," 358.
60. Harris, "Why Did Paul," 341.
61. Wolters, "Meaning," 66.
62. Wolters, "Meaning," 66.
63. Bowman, "Women in Ministry," 202. The word is used in the Pastorals in Titus 3:1 and is commonly used in its different constructions by Paul and Luke his likely amanuensis.
64. Harris, "Why Did Paul," 342.

very popular translation, the New International Version changing from positive in 1984 to negative in 2011.[65]

The word can also be translated "commit a murder!" It is argued that a similarly spelled word originated on its own with a different etymology, just as we have that phenomenon in English and we are rarely confused by it.[66] But equally, it can be an indication of a very negative connotation such as "'have full power and authority over' . . . [which would prevent] women from exercising an absolute power over men in such a way as to destroy them,"[67] Bowman suggests that "domineer or usurp authority" or simply "exercise authority" are both possible meanings for *authentein*, which were used during the New Testament period, but she concludes that "to exercise authority" may be preferable.[68] Another reading is simply "not domineer over her husband,"[69] which is very much a two-way street.

A very strong argument is made by Payne that its meaning is to "assume authority." He quotes John Werner who translated a papyrus from close to the time of Paul where his word is used and where its meaning is clear. There it is assumed authority. From that clear use, Werner concludes in relation to our passage that it "does not prevent a higher authority from delegating to a woman, equally as to a man, an authority to direct activities and/or to settle disputes involving them. When she exercises that authority, she will not be *authenteōing*: she will be exercising *exousia*."[70] Against this, is Schreiner who acknowledges about the meaning of *authenteō*, that "we should not rule out the possibility that the context might incline us toward the meaning 'domineer' or 'play the tyrant' rather than exercise authority."[71] However, he sees these

---

65. Burk, "New and Old," 280–87.
66. Wolters, "Meaning," 68.
67. Spencer, "Leadership," 8.
68. Bowman, "Women in Ministry," 202.
69. Barrett, *Pastoral*, 55.

70. Payne, *Man and Woman*, 366–67. The papyrus from 27/26 BC is an apology for one man assuming authority over another man's slave.

71. Schreiner, "Interpretation," 197.

words as only gaining meaning from his understanding of verses thirteen and fourteen which he believes favor exercising authority.

Verses eleven and twelve cannot be a blanket ban on women teaching, but rather permitting teaching in a situation where "their authority is properly recognised, not self-assumed."[72] Ultimately this is no different to men and he has already commanded certain men not to teach (1 Tim 1:3, 20). Paul saw teaching as an important function for all believers (Col 3:16). Elsewhere there was also no restriction on women teaching to build up the church (1 Cor 14:26). All the readers/hearers of Hebrews were also expected to be teachers. Perhaps this was of an informal nature, but there was never any explanation of this notion.[73] Teaching in the Pastorals implies a more authoritative action than other uses of "teaching" in the New Testament.[74] The authority here is linked closely with the realization that the sound doctrine of Christianity was still primarily oral,[75] but this would change substantially when it became written.

> **13** *For Adam was formed first, then Eve.* **14** *And Adam was not the one deceived; it was the woman who was deceived and became a sinner.* (NASB)

Verses 13 and 14. Could this thorny passage be no more than Paul refuting an amalgamation of Jewish-gnostic beliefs amalgamated with devotion to Artemis? We know from second-century sources that Gnosticism could hold that Eve was not a sinner or deceived and was created before Adam who was enlightened by her teaching. If correct, it would strengthen any argument that any restriction was only temporary.[76] Schreiner rejects this by arguing that sources from developed Gnosticism cannot be used to inform us about the nature of a developing error.[77] But should this pos-

---

72. Payne, *Man and Woman*, 359.
73. Saucy, "Women's Prohibition," 84.
74. Saucy, "Women's Prohibition," 91.
75. Saucy, "Women's Prohibition," 91.
76. Schreiner, "Interpretation," 165.
77. Schreiner, "Interpretation," 165.

sibility be discounted out of hand? Certainly not if the books are believed to be later than Paul.

Paul continues his restriction on woman's ministry by referring to Genesis chapters 2 and 3 but the logic for this prohibition is not immediately clear to many. The context has nothing to do with Eve being an official teacher or with Adam's authority.[78] Further, Paul had told the Corinthians that a woman being derived from a man has no more significance than that a man is born of a woman (1 Cor 11:11–12). By appealing to the rights of the firstborn (primogeniture), Paul takes this matter back to creation before the fall as the main authority and then reinforces this by appearing to lay blame for the fall with Eve. Elsewhere responsibility for the fall lies firmly with Adam (Rom 5:12–21; 1 Cor 15:21–22) and an apparent susceptibility of women to deception is not again in keeping with the Bible. The intensive form of the word "deceived" is used of Eve, i.e., utterly deceived, but she was, after all, deceived by the most cunning animal the Lord God had made (Gen 3:1). Eve simply had to offer the fruit to Adam, and he took it (Gen 3:6). If women were so likely to teach error, it would be grossly irresponsible to let them teach other women (Titus 2:3–5) and children (2 Tim 1:5; 3:15)! Because of educational opportunities denied or yet to be, they of all people had no way of determining if what they were being taught was correct! Rather, susceptibility to deception is a universal problem. Eve was "formed" by God, just as much as Adam was and to see some inherent weakness in a woman that is not there in a man is to denigrate the creator of both.

The mention of "deception," *epatēthē*, points us more to the action of the false teachers. Their deception had led many away from their faith (1 Tim 1:6, 9; 4:1; 5:15) and Paul uses language that links their activity to that of Satan (1 Tim 1:20; 3:6; 4:1; 5:15; 2 Tim 2:26). The disastrous consequences of Eve's deception are of a similar nature to the Ephesian women receiving and then passing on the satanic error. By treating Eve's deception as a cautionary

---

78. Harris, "Why Did Paul," 345.

type, it then applies in situations "where women are acting out of ignorance and being deceived."[79]

Adam and Eve is a paradigm suitable for Timothy who has mixed Jewish and Gentile blood. In the similar passage in 1 Peter, the Apostle uses Abraham and Sarah which would suit a predominately Jewish audience.[80] Despite only mentioning two verses from Genesis, it is claimed that this is a common rabbinic method of referring to the whole account of the creation of man and woman and their subsequent fall.[81] Man was created first and the Old Testament concept of the privileges that accrue to the firstborn were strong, including that of leading the family (Deut 21:15–17) and the double portion inheritance (v. 17). Yahweh's own practice in salvation history of rejecting the practice was stronger (Cain and Abel, Ishmael and Isaac, Esau and Jacob, Manasseh and Ephraim, and David and his brothers).[82] When this passage is examined as a whole, as is suggested, we also see that Eve was to be a helper comparable to Adam (Gen 2:20), not a hindrance and so not made for him to possess.[83] The need for a man and woman working together to make a whole was Paul's attitude also (1 Cor 11:11).

The possible reconstruction is that some Ephesian men were saying "look what has happened when we allowed women to attend our services and teach others." Or, "what else can we expect from women who are at heart sinners and need to be kept under strict discipline; all women are like Eve, inferior and sinners."[84] Paul accepted the analogy[85] that women of Ephesus were like Eve in that they were easily deceived and then misled others.[86] The issue is not

79. Harris, "Why did Paul," 350.
80. Hugenberger, "Women," 357.
81. Bowman, "Women in Ministry," 204–5.
82. Contra Gealy who says, "first is best." Gealy, "First," 406
83. Gealy, "First," 406.
84. Spencer, "Eve at Ephesus," 217; similarly Payne, "Libertarian," 188.
85. It is a simpler interpretation to say that this is a historical example (Payne, "Libertarian," 178) than to claim it is an anthropological norm. Moo, "1 Timothy 2:11–15," 68.
86. Payne, "Libertarian," 177.

that Eve was formed second, but that some Ephesian women were engaged in false teaching.[87] By reminding Timothy that it was Eve who was deceived and not Adam, Paul was not saying women are less intelligent and more easily deceived. They would have been more easily deceived simply because most had not been educated, which reflected on their social standing and not on themselves as people. If women were more easily deceived because of their gender it is surprising, as already mentioned, that Paul would allow them to teach other women as this would only compound the situation, Paul himself had been deceived by sin (Rom 7:11).

If Eve's fall came about through being deceived (note: she became a transgressor; she was not born that way), it must then follow that Adam's sin was deliberate![88] Eve at least had an excuse. With Adam sinning willfully, there would appear to be more of an argument in preventing men from preaching! The more so as Gen 3:6 reports Adam being present with Eve at the temptation and did not take the initiative of countering the serpent's lies.[89] Male spiritual leaders, far from being in a position of privilege, were placed in a position of enormous accountability because of their moral and spiritual failure. Again, it was men who were leading the Ephesian church astray and again it appears to be deliberate (1 Tim 1:20). In Genesis, no word of hope was given to the deliberately sinning male, but a promise was given to the woman, that there would be a descendant who would crush the serpent's head.

The women of Ephesus had listened to the false teachers, who like the snake, were the mouthpieces of Satan (1 Tim 4:1).[90] To these women was extended the promise of salvation, only the men had shipwrecked their faith (1 Tim 1:19–20). The resemblance to Eve may have been valid in Ephesus, but this

---

87. Payne, "Libertarian," 177.

88. Similarly, Payne, "Libertarian, 190.

89. Schreiner sees the temptation story as strengthening his argument for the subordinate role for women saying, "In approaching Eve, then, the Serpent subverted the pattern of male leadership and interacted only with the woman." Schreiner, "Interpretation," 215.

90. Padgett, "Wealthy Women," 26.

resemblance was not universal as Paul did not make this comparison with Phoebe, a female *prostatis* (helper) in the church. The Ephesian women would cease to be like Eve when they grew beyond error through learning and understanding the true faith.[91] It is a reasonable question to ask, should the restriction about teaching been more directed to men? In Paul's farewell to the Ephesian elders in Acts 20:13–35 he acknowledges that from among them, men who he appointed or at the very least allowed to stay in office, some were no better than savage wolves. This is much stronger than some women being deceived.

> **15** *But women will be saved through childbearing—if they continue in faith, love and holiness with propriety.*

Verse 15. Are women saved by childbearing[92] and men by grace through faith (Gal 3:28)? Is obedience to their "proper" role a necessity for women only? Possible meanings for this "very obscure"[93] verse are:

- They will be safely delivered through childbirth;[94]
- Women will be saved spiritually even though they must bear children;
- They will be saved spiritually equally with men by fulfilling their role in the home through childbearing[95] just as men will be by providing public church leadership;
- They will be kept safe from usurping men's leadership role by staying at home with the children; and
- They will be saved through faithfulness to their proper role as exemplified in motherhood.[96]

---

91. Spencer, "Eve at Ephesus," 221.

92. Moo maintains if faith, love, and holiness with propriety are conditions that demonstrate salvation, what is wrong with adding faithfulness to a God ordained role as another [evidence]. Moo, "Interpretation," 206.

93. Barrett, *Pastoral*, 56.

94. Alternative reading in the New English Bible.

95. Gealy, "First," 407.

96. Bowman, "Women in Ministry," 208.

Exposition of First Timothy 2:8-15

Paul's usage of *sózó*, "to save," in his letters refers to more than preservation in this world but Luke records him speaking it when being preserved from the shipwreck (Acts 27:30-31). This stops us quickly passing over the first option above and some do acknowledge this as a legitimate interpretation.[97] The role of Artemis in preserving a mother in childbirth has been mentioned in chapter 1 and a Christian mother should hope for and pray for no less. It would be expected that a pregnant woman's non-Christian friends would remind them of "savior Artemis." Some who were insecure in their faith may have had real fears about abandoning the vengeful god who provided safety in childbirth! This restrained and modest behavior certainly was in contrast to the intoxicated and wild practices seen in some of the religions in Ephesus. However, to see this verse as providing the key to a safe delivery is clearly wrong as Christian women have and still do die in childbirth.

The last of these options does not seem to address full salvation for woman that is to be found for them in Christ. In Christianity, women are saved equally and in the same way as men There is no place in the Christian church for the prayer "I thank God that I was not born a gentile or a woman."[98] But how can bearing children be associated with the Christian virtues of faith, love, and holiness? What does it mean in this context to be saved? Table 4 gives an indication of the broad spectrum of meanings for the concept of "saved" in Paul's writings.

Negatively	Positively
To rescue men from sin's	To bring men into a state of
a. Guilt Eph 1:7; Col 1:14	a. Righteousness Rom 3:21–26; 5:1
b. Slavery Rom 7:24–25; Gal 5:1	b. Freedom Gal 5:1; 2 Cor 3:17
c. Punishment through	c. Blessedness through

---

97. Barrett, *Pastoral*, 56–57.
98. Talmud, *Menahoth 43b–44*; Gritz, *Paul*, 21.

Negatively	Positively
1. Alienation from God Eph 2:12	1. Fellowship with God Eph 2:13
2. Wrath of God Rom Eph 2:3	2. The love of God shed abroad in the heart Rom 5:5
3. Everlasting death Eph 2:5–6	3. Everlasting life Eph 2:1,5; Col 3:1–4

Table 4. "Saved" in Paul's writings[99]

In this passage, the meaning is also ambiguous.[100] "Saved" is probably intended to take in the whole of the salvation life, with justification as its starting point and continuing with a life of holy living empowered by the Spirit (Rom 6:19; Gal 5:16; Phil 2:12–13; Col 1:10; 1 Thess 4:7). The conditions that give evidence of salvation are continuing in faith, love, and holiness with propriety. These are of quite a different order of things than having children. It can't be stressed enough; these women are not encouraged to acquire these things but to *continue* in them. These are the characteristics of people who *are* saved, not *will* be saved. Women's salvation will be consummated in their glorified state when they are presented to the Father in purity (Eph 5:26–27; Col 1:22; 1 Thess 3:13; 5:23). Again, this is no different to men.

While all the commentators acknowledge that women are saved by grace and not works, there can be a tendency to be inconsistent. While not all women will have children, that reference to childbearing is taken as representing the whole of what Paul refers to as "propriety." For instance, Schreiner says that Paul's purpose here, "is to say that women will not be saved if they do not practice good works."[101] Certainly, reference to childbirth was driven by the false teachers apparently denigrating marriage but it goes too far to say:

---

99. Hendriksen, *1&2 Thessalonians*, 79. Contra Fee who says "saved" only means redemption in the Pastorals. Fee, *1 and 2 Timothy*, 75.

100. Padgett, "Wealthy," 27.

101. Schreiner, "Interpretation, 223.

Exposition of First Timothy 2:8–15

The genuineness of salvation is evidenced not by childbirth alone but by a woman living a godly life and conforming to her God-ordained role. These good works are necessary to obtain eschatological salvation.[102]

Women (the writer has changed from the singular to the plural)[103] are saved *dia* childbirth,[104] generally meaning *by* rather than *through*. Paul has been talking about Eve in the previous two verses and nothing has indicated that the subject has returned primarily to the women of Ephesus except in the sense of how Eve was saved, so they shall be saved also. As the typology continues, the reference is to Gen 3:15 the *protoevangelium*, where the woman's seed would crush the head of the serpent. Could this be *the* childbearing? James Dunn, rejecting this interpretation as "far away from the point," maintains that Paul was saying that the pain of childbearing is a woman's part in the atonement in the primal sin.[105] Paul's whole ministry message is surely that Christ fulfilled this role. While Eve is an example of deception, she is also the example of salvation through bearing the seed.[106] The role of women in the fall has been balanced by their, not men's, role in salvation.[107] Any anthropological argument restricting their ministry has been balanced. Women were the victims in Ephesus but through Eve's seed extending from Seth through David to Christ, they would eventually know full salvation. While it is acknowledged as a valid interpretation, it does seem too vague to the average reader for

---

102. Schreiner, "Interpretation," 224

103. Padgett, "Wealthy, 27. This is a lapse according to Barrett. Barrett, *Pastoral*, 56.

104. Moo maintains that the rarity of the word makes it difficult to define this word precisely but there is lack of support for "childbearing." Moo, "Interpretation," 206.

105. Dunn, "First," 802.

106. Padgett, "Wealthy," 28. Barrett also sees this as an acceptable translation. Barrett, *Pastoral*, 56. Justin Martyr (c. 100–160) expresses a similar thought. Justin, "Dialogue," 100. Contra Fee who, denying *protoevangelium's* existence, argues that there is no circumstance under which it could be interpreted as Mary's child. Fee, *1 and 2 Timothy*, 75.

107. Payne, "Libertarian," 179, 181.

this to actually be what Paul was referring to in this case. Against this Timothy was theologically trained and knew Paul's mind. And really, what we have in the private letter could almost be described as one side of a telephone conversation. Whatever he meant, this is exactly what happened for both men and women.

The meaning of *salvation by/through childbirth* was not all spiritual. The deceived wealthy women of Ephesus had followed false teachers who had taught that marriage was tainted (1 Tim 4:3).[108] To return to the marriage bed was a rejection of the snake-like false teachers. Padgett describes this salvation saying, "Woman's role in creation and salvation is a glorious and honorable one. By accepting this role, and thus rejecting the false teachers, these women will be saved from the snake."[109] But it was not enough to be delivered from this deception, they also had to be saved, but here not as an eschatological event but a process in this life. This process involved leaving the false teachers and living instead in faith, love, and holiness. Eve's role then was not just as a cautionary type but also as a positive example. There is nothing in these passages that would limit the role of women in the present church.[110]

3:1 Here is a trustworthy saying (NASB).

Paul's reliable opinion could either be read at the conclusion of his directions about women or his introduction to church officers.

---

108. This was to be a feature of later Gnosticism. A similar attitude is seen throughout the *Acts of Paul and Thecla*.
109. Padgett, "Wealthy," 29.
110. Padgett, "Wealthy," 30.

4

Bringing the Threads Together

Authorship of the Pastoral Epistles

THE SUBJECT OF AUTHORSHIP brings uncomfortable questions about the traditional understanding of biblical authority. Hundreds of millions of Christians are oblivious to and care nothing for questions of who wrote First and Second Timothy and Titus as, for most, the question of canonicity and authority is the same. They believe these books to be the inspired and revealed word of God written by Paul and helpful for Christian living. For the Catholic Church, "the criterion of canonicity is acceptance into the Vulgate."[1] Acceptance by Jerome in his translation would not be sufficient for the Protestants who require different criteria. For many, the sole criterion is simply whether it is part of the King James Bible.[2] Others, who are informed about the problems of authorship, are content to let the matter rest with

---

1. Brown, *John I–XII*, 336.

2. Brown, *Introduction*, 336. It is difficult to say how much Brown oversimplifies. There is a reverence for the Authorized Version beyond which it now deserves.

church confessions.[3] For others, the question is meaningless, or even an affront to Christianity as talk of any "preconceived notion of 'inspiration' . . . will not bear examination when confronted with the facts."[4]

What are the implications for accepting pseudonymity when nine of the New Testament books are either anonymous or vaguely identified? Whereas the message of the anonymous books stands even if our understanding of the authorship is in error, the Pastoral Epistles are different, as they claim Pauline authorship, i.e., they may be built on a lie. Raymond Brown puts the matter clearly by saying, "It is hard to see, however, how a proposal that the writer of the Pastorals was intentionally deceptive and consciously desired to counteract[5] Paul's genuine heritage can be fitted into any notion of inspiration, even a sophisticated one."[6]

Brown speculates that even with pseudonymity, it may be possible to accept inspiration and still reject revelation. This is much the same as interpreting historical narrative where the story is generally told without comment. We are left to make up our own mind if it is a good or bad example.[7] In the same way, we are to make up our own mind about what is said in the Pastoral Epistles. Do they show a system "destructive of the personal worth of women?"[8] If these books do show repression and if the books are revealed, then we also can oppress women. In fact, it becomes our duty to do so! As one advocate of the complementary view said, "For those who hold a high view of biblical authority, the text must reign over and correct what we think is 'fair.'"[9] If it is just an inspired document, we can learn from it that God does not want us

---

3. "I am aware of the problems of authorship but as a Lutheran pastor I am obliged to believe that the letters are Paul's." Liebelt, Eric. *Pers. Com.* 2006.

4. Guy, *Gospel of Mark*, 2.

5. Some radical authorship theories see the writer correcting the Pauline heritage. Brown, *Introduction*, 663.

6. Brown, *Introduction*, 667–68.

7. Fee and Stuart, *How to Read*, 78.

8. Brown, *Introduction*, 668.

9. Schreiner, "Interpretation," 214.

to oppress women because it is not in his nature to do so. Such an understanding of the Pastoral Epistles would cause us to be more careful about framing the church in the social setting it is found.[10] After all, for all his virtues, Paul was not infallible, that was the role of Jesus. For his part Paul appears to have an anger management problem (Acts 15:39; Gal 2:11–21).

How we assess the authority of the Pastoral Epistles in relation to women's ministry cannot be separated from authorship. If Pauline authorship is rejected, it is difficult to see the books as ultimately being any more authoritative or reliable than *The Acts of Paul and Thecla*. There a woman had a preaching ministry alongside Paul.

Culture

Rick Strelan summarizes the situation for women in Ephesus as:

> With Artemis they "belonged"—they were part of the city, its cult, its traditions, and its wealth; with Demeter, they were associated with the cycle of death and life, production and reproduction, and so had power (even magical) on the estates and outlying farms and gardens of the city, as they planted and nurtured crops; with Dionysus they were able to transgress the barriers between marriage and virginity, between male and female, between humans and the gods.[11]

Considering the vitality and belonging those women were experiencing in the rival cults to Christianity, Dunn's observations in relation to women's attire are sobering. He observes that if the husband was alive, then expensive clothing could only be purchased with his permission. This extravagance could have come from an attempt to find satisfaction in such apparel. He remarks, "A religion that saw its end result in such terms would be no more

---

10. Brown, *Introduction*, 668.
11. Strelan, *Paul*, 125.

than a club for social advancement."[12] This would surely have been a travesty of all that was intended for women.

The suppression of women's ministry can be argued from the Greek culture of the day. William Barclay describes their position, "The respectable Greek woman led a very confined life. She lived in her own quarters into which no one but her husband came. She did not even appear at mealtimes. She never at any time appeared on the street alone; she never went to any public assembly."[13] Any book that simply reflects cultural values at a given time cannot be authoritative. It is well to remember that "stabilized piety"[14] for generations defended slavery, child labor, slums, and racial discrimination.[15] Male dominated, or male only ministry, is not in keeping with a modern attitude, which moves steadily toward the equality of the sexes insofar as rights and privileges are concerned.[16] Morgan Noyes questions whether these changes have come "under the pressure of the spirit of Christ"? Do we have, as he further asserts, "a case where an early Christian understanding of the will of God needs to be corrected by the further light which God has caused to break forth from his word?"[17]

Yet Noyes' claims do not adequately recognize that Paul's own teaching seems to be radically contradictory to this cultural ban. Christ has made us one, breaking down the dividing walls (Eph 2:14). There is no longer any division between groups of people but only whether they are in Christ (Col 3:1) extending even to the division of male and female (Gal 3:28).

---

12. Dunn, "First," 801.
13. Barclay, *Letters to Timothy*, 67.
14. Noyes, "First and Second Epistles," 407.
15. Noyes, "First and Second Epistles," 407.
16. Noyes, "First and Second Epistles," 407.
17. Noyes, "First and Second Epistles," 406–7.

Bringing the Threads Together

Authority

In the Jewish rabbinic system, teachers drew men under their authority, molding them into their image.[18] This compares with the authority of Jesus as the teacher and rabbi for Christians (Matt 23:8). When a rabbinical style teacher–pupil relationship developed in Corinth, Paul denounced it (1 Cor 1:10–17).[19] In this sense, Paul would not have allowed men to have authority over men either. There were different levels of authority among the teachers, with Jesus being the ultimate authority, and authority decreasing through the apostles, to the teachers in the church and eventually to the individual believer.[20] And all of this is based on servanthood.

While restrictions on women exercising authority have been an undoubted cultural practice, it is argued that there is no verse in the scriptures, other than 1 Tim 2:8–15, which states (apparently) that women are never to be in authority over men.[21] My argument that too much relies on the disputed meaning of a single verse is supported by the Old Testament example of Deborah, who, with God's gifting and blessing, rose to the highest position in Israel. This would not have been possible if "women in every age and place are not suited to teach or have authority over men."[22] Women were also used to speak/write key portions of the scriptures, e.g., Eve, Miriam, Deborah, Ruth, Esther, Anna, Mary, and Elizabeth. Looking to Old Testament practice of how they were treated should not be confused with how they should have been treated. Miriam is specifically said to have been sent to lead Israel (Mic 6:4) and Deborah was raised up by the Lord (Judg 2:16, 18). In fact, they held all positions of authority excluding that of priest. The great prophesy of Joel about Christ's kingdom sees a much-expanded role for women, not a diminished one (Joel 2:28; Acts 2:14–21)!

---

18. Saucy, "Women's Prohibition," 83.
19. Saucy, "Women's Prohibition," 83.
20. Saucy, "Women's Prohibition," 85.
21. Payne, "Libertarian," 176.
22. Payne, "Libertarian," 185.

Women in Ministry

It is hard to imagine that the considerable help Paul's female coworkers provided did not involve a spoken ministry (Rom 16:2; Phil 4:2–3) and in Priscilla's case, an advanced knowledge of theology. There was clearly a significant spoken ministry by women in the New Testament church. Largely on the basis of 1 Tim 2:12, the overall biblical picture and their present role in conservative churches frequently do not match. Prophecy was also an important part of the female ministry. If Paul had advised all Christians that they should seek the gift of prophecy, are women now sinning if they still desire to speak for Him? If it is claimed that this role is not available to women, as this pneumatic ministry has ceased, a corresponding role must be given to women![23] The lack of women in leadership roles need not be evidence of the Spirit guiding the church but may rather be that of the church quenching the Spirit!

Overseers should have been able to teach (1 Tim 3:2), but there was no requirement that they have the spiritual gift of teaching,[24] nor does it state that they were the only ones to teach. In the New Testament church, it was intended that every member should be involved in teaching (Eph 4:12). Priscilla and Aquila had been left in Ephesus after Paul's initial work, apparently to oversee the work. As mentioned in chapter 2, the pair were active in ministry and Paul called them his "fellow workers" (Rom 16:3–4). They both instructed Apollos (Acts 18:26), which was exactly what was claimed to be forbidden by the Pastoral Epistles. Is teaching just the spoken word in the assembly or does it cover saying exactly the same thing in a hymn or a theological work? The church is not consistent here.

It is questioned whether teaching and having authority are two separate activities or are one related action, as in exercising authority over those being taught. There is no agreement on this, and both are quite possible.[25] If the latter meaning is correct then women are not forbidden to teach, just to have the ultimate

---

23. Saucy, "Women's Prohibition," 80.

24. Payne, "Libertarian," 174.

25. E.g., Payne argues that "teaching" and "having authority" is not the same act. Payne, "Libertarian," 176.

Bringing the Threads Together

authority. Women's ministry frequently falls far short of even this. If the issue is whether a woman can teach or not, it questions her intellect and spiritual reliability.[26] This simply falls short of experience in societies where women are now well educated. Payne puts the argument clearly saying, "It is precarious indeed to deny that women should never be in a position of authority over men based on the disputed meaning of *authenteō* especially considering the only occurrence of this word anywhere in the Bible."[27]

For many women, learning in silence would have led to a situation where they would have "at least the ability to become authoritative teachers."[28] Did Paul intend women to always remain at the early stage of spiritual growth as we see in Ephesus, or should they be encouraged to reach their potential? Kent is typical of those who limit the role of women. He sees no public outlet for what they have learned, basing his argument on the meaning of *didaskein*, in 1 Tim 2:12, which is in the present tense, meaning to be a teacher, not an aorist, meaning to teach. First Corinthians 6:2–3 sees women as becoming the judges of the world as well as angels but even this does not convince him that women can be the authoritative bearers of doctrine in this age.[29] The significance of the word is accepted but not the conclusion as it misses the significance of the context. Paul does not have in mind a permanent ban on women teachers,[30] but just these women, as he uses *epitrepō* (the first person present), "I do not permit," not the aorist.[31] The aorist is a tense not found in Latin or Germanic languages and would indicate an action that took place at one point in time. When properly instructed there was no reason for them not to serve at least as deacons,[32] i.e., apprentice elders, in the early Ephesian church.

26. Keener, *Paul*, 240.
27. Payne, "Libertarian," 176.
28. Spencer, "Eve at Ephesus," 220.
29. Kent, *Pastoral*, 113.
30. Payne, "Libertarian," 172.
31. Padgett, "Wealthy," 25; Spencer, "Eve at Ephesus," 220.
32. Padgett, "Wealthy," 25.

Women in Ministry

The existence of female *diakonoi* does not mean that their role was the same as the men. Using the model of the church being the family of God, it would have required the woman, like the wife, to have "status and religious obligations."[33] It is suggested that the family model of the church would have pressured the women to concentrate their ministries in the domestic arena and so vanish from the scene as a distinct group.[34] While it may explain, it does not justify a diminished role of women in ministry.

Paul had shown that he was willing to compromise on peripheral issues such as when he circumcised Timothy to keep harmony with the Jews (Acts 16:2). It is quite possible that, as the church settled in for the long haul, and with the passing of the apostles and men like Timothy and Titus, that the eschatological fervor of the original message began to wane. Bart Ehrman suggests that "the Roman ideology of gender relationships became Christianized, and the social implications of Paul's apocalyptic vision became lost."[35] On the other hand it is argued that "the revisionist" view only coincides with the feminist movement with the first paper occurring in 1969 followed by a flood of articles.[36] This view would see that by rejecting 1900 years of tradition, we are accepting the spirit of the age when it should be resisted.[37] It can be equally argued that for 1,900 years the male leaders of the church did not resist the spirit of their age.[38] Those who seek to restrict the teaching role of women must provide much clearer scriptural

---

33. Pietersen, *Polemic*, 114.
34. Stiefel, "Women," 456.
35. Mappes, "Moral Virtues," 203–19.
36. Hughes, "Living Out," 103.
37. Hughes, "Living Out," 104.
38. Perhaps the Puritans were right when they said, "there is yet more light and truth to break forth from His word."

evidence[39] as so much hinges on verses that do not "constitute clear evidence."[40]

No Episcopal System

The words used in the Pastoral Epistles to describe the officers of the church, bishop, and presbyters/elders and deacons, have become familiar to us through the episcopal system of Catholicism. This church has a totally male priesthood. It is far from certain that the terms of the modern episcopal system mean the same as they did in the first century. Frequently the terms bishop and presbyter, as used in the Pastoral Epistles are seen not as separate offices but rather the one group with the bishop being "the president of the college of elders."[41] Ignatius (whose death occurred between 98–117) in his letter argues so strongly for the episcope[42] that it suggests that the role was not universally accepted.

I can see nothing in First and Second Timothy to support a male dominated episcopal ministry. Rather it projects a positive role for women's ministry once trained accurately in the gospel.

Women as Example

Timothy and Titus provided examples of what Christ was like to churches troubled with heresy. When Paul wanted to encourage Timothy (and himself) in this difficult role (2 Tim 1:6–7), he did this through using memories. The aged apostle remembered Timothy (2 Tim 1:3), his tears (2 Tim 1:4), his sincere faith (2 Tim 1:5), but he also encouraged him with memories of his mother and grandmother (2 Tim 1:5). We find a paradigm for Christian

---

39. Traditional scholars say that it the revisionists that have to *prove* their case. Moo, "Interpretation," 196, 209; Hughes, "Living Out," 103. I believe the minimum the revisionists have to establish is *reasonable doubt* based on unclear texts.
40. Moo, "Interpretation," 201.
41. Pietersen, *Polemic, 98*.
42. Ignatius, *Smyrn.* 8.

encouragement in Second Timothy 1:6–14.[43] The Spirit dwells in all Christians, not just the elite leaders such as Paul and Timothy. Paul pointed to the example of a grandmother or a mother as an encouragement for correct Christian living. Through the Spirit, the ordinary, even an ordinary woman, can become extraordinary.

Women in Genesis 1–3

A further implication for the extent of Christian salvation also follows if we consider again the Genesis account that Paul has used in 1 Tim 2:13–14. Genesis 1:26–28, referring to the pre-fall area, asserted "the spiritual equality of woman and man—both made in the image of God. It also recognizes that two share the same responsibilities with regard to the created universe."[44] After the fall, in Gen 3:16, the woman did not escape the penalty of her sin: her pain in childbirth was greatly increased and her relation to her husband had changed. Formerly her husband's response was to love and cherish her but in a fallen world this has too often turned to desire and domination. In Jesus' teaching on divorce, he went back to the conditions before the fall to rule that the permission in the Law to divorce was a concession to a hard heart rather than the pattern to be followed by his disciples.

In ancient households, man was the head of the house with ultimate authority. The family was the basic unit of city and state and women had to play a submissive role (Eph 5:22; Col 3:18).[45] Most churches were in private homes so there may have been uncertainty over whether the household or the church was the norm for behavior.[46] Dunn gives the example of a wife prophesying or using other gifts in a house church and so could have been seen to be teaching her husband.[47] He argues that the church was made

43. Mounce, *Pastoral Epistles*, 490.
44. Gritz, *Paul*, 55.
45. Dunn, "First," 801.
46. Dunn, "First," 801.
47. Dunn, "First," 801.

Bringing the Threads Together

to conform to the family so as to be seen as supporting an ordered society. In a Christian home, where members believed they have been redeemed from the curse referred to in 1 Tim 2:13–15, the fall could no longer be the model for husband/wife relations. In a Christian home, desire and domination should have been replaced with the original loving and cherishing nature of the husband where both treat one another in honor (Eph 5:21; 1 Cor 11:11–12). In Christ, the great divides between different groups of people and between the sexes have been broken down (Col 3:11; Eph 2:14; 5:21; 1 Cor 11:11–12; Gal 3:28).

The Role of Women

It is hard to see the apostolic church as being anything other than primarily a lay organization where all were expected to play a part (1 Cor 14:26) and where women played a leading and varied role. It was a place where the "Spirit would descend without regard to sex."[48] But by placing the life situation of the Pastoral Epistles later than that of the apostolic period, we would have a situation where some "women were seeking release, vocation and status [which] could not have allowed the old ways to go unchallenged."[49] Gealy surmises that despite some men agreeing to this, the practice had to stop.[50] If this assessment of women's ministry is correct, then there is an inconsistency in the faith as it promoted a freedom for women, which in turn had to be stifled.

The problem of women's ministry as it is traditionally understood is that "First Timothy seems inconsistent with the contemporary achievements of women or the concept of a loving God."[51] It also seems inconsistent with the very impressive list of women who had worked in ministry with Paul (Rom 16). Ten women were affirmed by Paul, with two of these being so involved in missionary

---

48. Gealy, "First," 403.
49. Gealy, "First," 403.
50. Gealy, "First," 403.
51. Spencer, "Eve at Ephesus," 216.

work that they had been imprisoned. Though the greater number of those in the evangelical tradition follow the restrictive historical view,[52] it is possible to hold a more liberal view arguing on the basis of the accepted exegetical methodology.

The qualifications for leadership are rather general and not exceptional[53] considering most of them are virtues that every believer, female and male, minister and layman, should possess.[54] Table 2 shows that exactly the same requirements are expected of all women that are set for the overseer. It seems very unfair to demand standards of all women, even young widows, which were qualities that most men probably did not possess. It is unjust to suggest that when women achieved this standard, there was not the same outlet for this maturity and knowledge as for men. How is this fundamentally different to the caste system that says it is better for a person to be working poorly in his/her caste than that person do the task well outside of their caste? With the troubles in the church arising from the elders, it is not surprising that as much care was taken in the appointment of deacons as it was for elders. These men (and women?) were the future of the church and are a reminder that ministry is concerned with generations, not months or years.

But with Paul's imminent death and the foreseeable departure and eventual death of his companions, the model of authoritative apostles and delegates would soon pass. Church officers had progressed from imitating the apostles to being the examples themselves. This imitation was not a two-tiered arrangement with a lesser standard for members based on office or gender. Imitation is at the core of the Lord's Prayer and is far more radical than anything Paul said. In the prayer there is no imitation of Christ, or an apostle but the Father is asked to imitate the believer.[55] This high

---

52. Hughes, "Living," 102.

53. Moo, "Interpretation," 212.

54. Moo, "Interpretation," 212.

55. Gregory of Nyssa graphically illustrated this point saying, "Jesus wants your disposition to be a good example to God. We invite God to imitate us. Do thou the same as I have done. Imitate thy servant O Lord. Though he be only a poor beggar and thou art the King of the universe. I have shown great mercy to my neighbour imitate thy servant's charity." Barclay, *Lord's Prayer*, 95.

Bringing the Threads Together

standard of a life that is to be imitated is expected of all believers; women are not exempted and men are not exempted from imitating women's example.

Women had already fulfilled the requirements of apostleship—they had been witnesses of Jesus' life, ministry, and resurrection. Jesus sent women out to proclaim the good news when he sent them to tell the apostles, despite the laws that refused to accept a woman's testimony.[56] Any argument about a male bias by Jesus' choosing the twelve has limited value. Jesus did not choose any gentiles either.[57]

Exposition

Paul wrote in Gal 3:28, "There is neither Jew nor Greek, there is neither slave nor free, there is neither male nor female; for you are all one in Christ Jesus" (NASB). This is sharply contrary to the formula whereby a Jewish male would thank God each morning that he has not been born a gentile, a slave, or a woman. The greatest barrier of all these was between Jew and Gentile. This should not have been a disparagement of these three groups as lesser persons but a recognition that they "were excluded from religious privileges only open to Jewish males."[58] He also firmly stood against circumcision, which would have established a male-only level of membership in the church.[59] While their roles may remain on social grounds, in the family of the church these divisions were irrelevant. With leadership open to Gentiles and slaves, and the recognized role of women laboring beside Paul and his acknowledgement of their right to pray and prophesy, why can't a woman minister as freely as a man? F. F. Bruce puts his position clearly: "Paul states the basic principle here: if restrictions on [women's ministry] are found elsewhere in the Pauline corpus as in . . . 1

- 56. Gritz, *Paul*, 77.
- 57. Gritz, *Paul*, 77.
- 58. Bruce, *Galatians*, 187.
- 59. Johnson, *First and Second*, 206.

Tim 2:11f., they are to be understood in relation to Gal 3:28, and not *vice versa*."[60]

The accusation is that this creates a cannon within a cannon with preferred texts coming to prominence and all but ignoring unwelcome ones. This can make the task of interpretation highly subjective.[61] This approach could be dismissed if this is the only area where it occurs![62] Both passages may be equally inspired, but the widely divergent interpretations show that they are not equally clear. Even supporters of the traditional view would generally not argue that missionary activity, which has relied heavily on the involvement of women, has suffered as a consequence. As one critic of women's ministry said, "The facts on the ground appear to speak for themselves."[63] We are in danger of substituting the great Jew/Gentile divide with male/female instead. Paul wanted to promote liberation and, for the "first-century women at Ephesus, learning the knowledge of God's truth from the appropriate persons was liberating."[64] But after almost 2,000 years, with teaching opportunities never envisaged in the first century, simply learning without a release is not liberating. The interpretation of 1 Tim 2:11–15 that I suggest does not require a complete and ongoing opposition by Paul to women's ministry. Spencer, looking at the totality of the apostle's attitude to women's ministry states:

> If anything, the development of Paul's work at Ephesus should culminate in the authoritative leadership of schooled orthodox women today. Paul never meant for women to remain at the beginning stage of growth exemplified by women at Ephesus. It was his design to have them mature as heirs according to God's promise (Galatians 3:26–29). Thus, he would rejoice to see Galatians 3:28 become a reality in our actions.[65]

60. Bruce, *Galatians*, 190.
61. Duinkerken, "Women," 347.
62. The Calvinist/Arminian debate is a case in point.
63. Bray, *Pastoral*, 175.
64. Spencer, "Eve at Ephesus," 221.
65. Spencer, "Eve at Ephesus," 221–22.

Bringing the Threads Together

While 1 Tim 2:11–15 is used to justify women's limited ministry, in practice the church frequently finds itself in a situation where it pays lip service to restrictions but then finds ways to circumvent it. For instance, some see it as acceptable for a woman to teach a man on the mission field when there is a male head of mission.[66] Using this argument, there were no problems with women's ministry in Ephesus, as it was the mission field![67]

Non-Pauline authorship demands that these verses were written to "withstand the mighty assault of syncretistic and ascetic tendencies and movements."[68] This would be a time of retreat into "stabilized piety,"[69] when Spirit phenomena had virtually ceased and there has been a reaction to the extravagances of the emancipation of women.[70] This all but demands women's ministry in Paul's time.

---

66. Kent, *Pastoral*, 114.

67. The order of the great commission was Jerusalem, Judea, Samaria, and the uttermost parts of the world.

68. Dibelius and Conzelmann, *Pastoral*, 49.

69. Gealy, "First," 405.

70. Gealy, "First," 405.

Conclusion

ENVISAGE THE SCENE THAT must have happened many times. A pastor carries the suitcase of a young godly female missionary down to the dock to bid her farewell as she departs for places unknown, and too often to her death. Yet, driven by the dogmatism that surrounds 1 Tim 2:8–15, this woman was not allowed to pray, let alone teach, in the church that commissioned her. Does First and Second Timothy commend or condemn this pastor and his church?

When assessing the role of women in ministry in First and Second Timothy, we are confronted with questions that cannot be answered easily or with certainty. Who wrote these books? While Orthodoxy demands it was Paul, scholars are deeply divided. Even if Pauline authorship is accepted, are the instructions of an unmarried male rabbi to an ancient society of relevance in a modern world? Educated women have proven themselves equal to men in secular spheres. Are the Pastoral Epistles authoritative, even if inspiration is accepted? How dogmatic should we be about 1 Tim 2:8–15, which appears to be very unclear with its use of complex words and a flow of thought that is not clear? Yet dogmatism is exactly what has characterized this passage.

Women in Ministry

When the Temple of Artemis was finally uncovered, it was found six meters under the surface of the swamp on which it was built. That city's gods and its wild religious practices have passed away and are now just a curiosity. I have attempted to show that the life situation confronted by Paul and Timothy has little relevance to a modern church setting. The New Testament church was plagued with error and would continue to be plagued with errors. One obvious change that has occurred in the church since New Testament times is that women are now educated and are seen as the equal of men in today's society. While many women in Ephesus had come straight out of Paganism, many women are now likely to have grown up in the faith and have been taught correctly its doctrines and way of life. There is little that now connects them to the ancient world.

In Luke 13:10–17, Jesus showed his readiness and courage to upset religious sensibilities by healing on the Sabbath so that "a daughter of Abraham, whom Satan bound for eighteen long years, be set free from this bondage on the Sabbath day." "Daughters of Abraham" have been bound in church settings for almost 2,000 years and many would say they need to be freed so they can achieve "release, vocation, and status."[1] The strong move for ordination of women in churches that have traditionally denied women's ministry is evidence of this. Paul's call to Christians was to freedom (2 Cor 3:17; Gal 5:1). This was not just to a nebulous "spiritual" freedom but, as the opportunity arose, real tangible freedom. If Paul advised a slave to obtain his freedom if the opportunity arose (1 Cor 7:21), how can women be considered any different? To be denied the validity of Spirit-given gifts through neglect or force, can only be seen as enslavement not freedom.

Their role could be different if women are, by nature, sinful, easily deceived, and capable of leading their husbands into sin. Though it is suggested that some in Ephesus held this view, I have attempted to show that Paul went out of his way to counter this view. How great a salvation was being offered in Christianity? Was it salvation that could draw a line of forgiveness under

---

1. Gealy, "First," 403.

Conclusion

Adam's intentional sin when he knew what he was doing, yet not under Eve's deception? Was there a greater salvation for men than for women who were not quite redeemed and not quite forgiven? Rather than following the role model of Eve, one which was to be avoided, the Pastoral Epistles picture women with a faith so deep that Paul uses them as role models for him and Timothy to follow. As the Lord's Prayer teaches, women could (and should) possess a character of godliness so deep that it urges God to imitate them.

There is no place, on the basis of First and Second Timothy, for dogmatically excluding half of the church from reaching their full potential in ministry. While society has changed dramatically since ancient Ephesus, the criteria that we see from First and Second Timothy for ministry remain the same:

- Depth of character, with no lesser standards for women than men,
- A sound knowledge of the faith, and
- A natural ability to teach.

Added to this, but not essential, is a Spirit enabled gift of teaching. When this criterion is present who can question the wisdom of the gift giver who gives as he chooses?

In the final washup, the role of apostle and prophet have long gone from the consciousness of most churches. While that of elder and deacon continue in name their roles are not always the same from church to church. Complicating the matter further, there are now areas of ministry not envisaged in the Ephesian setting. The church now must address the role of women in a much broader arena as Sunday school superintendent, worship leader, chairwomen of a board, etc. It also must address areas where men will not take up a leadership role. In many settings, strict compliance with the traditional reading of authority from First Timothy chapter 2 would make Christian ministry simply unviable. In the early chapters of Acts many believers were scandalized by who the gospel was to be preached to: eunuchs, Godfearers, and irreligious gentiles, let alone women. God's good name had to be protected from such obvious breaches of what was accepted as right and normal. For many in this age the scandal is now who proclaims this message.

Bibliography

Aelian. *Historical Miscellany*. Cambridge: Harvard University Press, 1997.
Antipater of Sidon. *The Greek Anthology*. Vol. 3, Book 9, "The Declamatory Epigrams," 396–97. Translated by W. R. Paton. Loeb Classical Library 84. London: William Heineman, 1943.
Apollodoros. "Apollodorus Against Nearia: [Demosthenes] 59." In *Greek Orators VI*. Translated and edited by Christopher Carey. Warminster: Aris and Phillips, 1992.
Appian. *The Foreign Wars*. Edited by Horace White. Loeb Classical Library 3. New York: Macmillan, 1899.
Aristides, P. Aelius. *P. Aelius Aristides, The Complete Works*. Vol. 1. Translated by Charles A. Behr. Leiden: E.J. Brill, 1981.
Arnold, Clinton E. *Ephesians: Power and Magic, The Concept of Power in Ephesians in Light of its Historical Setting*. Cambridge: Cambridge University Press, 1989.
Athenaeus Naucratita. *The Deipnosophists*. Vol. 6. Translated by Charles Burton Gulick. Loeb Classical Library 327. Cambridge: Harvard University Press, 1959.
Augustus Caesar. *The Deeds of Divine Augustus*. Translated by Thomas Bushnell. http://classics.mit.edu/Augustus/deeds.html.
Barclay, William. *Ambassador for Christ*. Edinburgh: St. Andrew, 1973.
———. *Ethics in a Permissive Society*. London: Fontana, 1971.
———. *The Letters to Timothy, Titus and Philemon*. Sydney: Christian, 1987.
———. *The Lord's Prayer*. Westminster: John Knox, 1998.
Barrett, C. K. *The Pastoral Epistles*. Oxford: Oxford University Press, 1963.

Bibliography

Baugh, S. M. "Cult Prostitution in New Testament Ephesus: A Reappraisal." *Journal of the Evangelical Theological Society* 42.3 (1999) 443–60.

———. "A Foreign World, Ephesus in the First Century." In *Women in the Church: An Interpretation and Application of 1 Timothy 2:9–15*, edited by Andreas J. Kostenberger and Thomas R. Schreiner, 25–64. 3rd edition. Wheaton, IL: Crossway, 2016.

Belleville, Linda L. "Chapter 2." In *Two Views on Women in Ministry*, edited by James R. Beck and Craig L. Bloomberg, 77–154. Grand Rapids: Zondervan, 2001.

Bowman, Anne L. "Chapter 4." In *Two Views on Women in Ministry*, edited by James R. Beck and Craig L Bloomberg, 237–302. Grand Rapids: Zondervan, 2001.

———. "Women in Ministry: An Exegetical Study of 1 Timothy 2:11–15." *Bibliotheca Sacra* 149 (1992) 194–214.

Bray, Gerald L. *The Pastoral Epistles*. London: T and T Clark, 2019.

Brough, S. M. "The Apostle among the Amazons." In *Westminster Theological Journal* 56 (1994) 154–72.

Brown, Raymond E. *The Gospel According to John I–XII*. Anchor Bible Series 29. New York: Doubleday, 1966.

———. *An Introduction to the New Testament*. Anchor Bible Reference Library Series. New York: Doubleday, 1997.

Bruce, F. F. *The Epistle to the Galatians*. Exeter: Paternoster, 1982.

———. *The Spreading Flame*. London: Paternoster, 1966.

Bultmann, Rudolph. "γινώσκω, γνῶσις, ἐπιγινώσκω, ἐπίγνωσις." In *Theological Dictionary of the New Testament*, edited by G. Kittel, G. W. Bromiley, and G. Friedrich, 1.689–719. Grand Rapids: Eerdmans, 1964.

Burk, Danny. "New and Old Departures in the Translation of αὐθεντεῖν in 1 Timothy 2:12." In *Women in the Church: An Interpretation and Application of 1 Timothy 2:9–15*, edited by Andreas J. Kostenberger and Thomas R. Schreiner, 279–96. 3rd edition. Wheaton, IL: Crossway, 2016.

Callimachus. *Callimachus Hymns and Epigrams*. Translated by C. A. Trypanis. Loeb Classical Library 129. London: William Heineman, 1986.

Clement. "First Epistle." In *The Ante-Nicene Fathers*. Vol. 8, *Translations of the Writings of the Fathers Down to A.D. 325. Fathers of the Third and Fourth Centuries: The Twelve Patriarchs, Excerpts and Epistles, The Clementina, Apocrypha, Decretals, Memoirs of Edessa and Syriac Documents, Remains of the First Ages*. Edited by A. Roberts, et al. Oak Harbor, WA: Logos Research Systems, 1997.

———. "First Epistle to the Corinthians." In *The Ante-Nicene Fathers*. Vol. 1, *Translations of the Writings of the Fathers down to A.D. 325. The Apostolic Fathers with Justin Martyr and Irenaeus*. Edited by A. Roberts, et al., 1–22. Oak Harbor, WA: Logos Research Systems, 1997.

Clement of Alexandria. "Stromata Book 3." In *The Library of Christian Classics*. Vol. 2, *Alexandrian Christianity: Selected Translations of Clement and Origin*, 40–92. Philadelphia: Westminster, 1954.

Bibliography

Culver, Robert D. "A Traditional View: Let Your Women Keep Silence." In *Women in Ministry, Four Views*, edited by Bonnidell Clouse and Robert G. Clouse, 25–52. Downers Grove, IL: Intervarsity, 1989.

De Welt, Don. *Paul's Letters to Timothy and Titus*. Joplin, MO: College, 1981.

Dibelius, Martin, and Hans Conzelmann. *The Pastoral Epistles*. Philadelphia: Fortress, 1972.

Dio, Cassius Cocceianus. "Roman History." In *Dio's Roman History*, vols. 6 and 7, translated by Earnest Cary. Loeb Classical Library 32. London: William Heinemann, 1955.

Dio Chrysostom. "The Thirty First Discourse to the People of Rhodes." In *Dio Chrysostom*, vol. 3, translated by J. W. Cohoon and H. Lamar Crosby. Loeb Classical Library 358. London: William Heineman, 1951.

Duinkerken, André. "Women in the Pauline Mission." In *The Gospel to the Nations*, edited by Peter G. Bolt and Mark D. Thompson, 221–47. Leicester: InterVarsity, 2000.

Dunn, James D. G. "The First and Second Letters to Timothy and the Letter to Titus." In *The New Interpreters Bible*, vol. 11, edited by Leander E. Keck et. al., 775–880. Nashville: Abingdon, 2000.

Earle, Ralph. "1 Timothy and 2 Timothy." In *The Expositors Bible Commentary*, vol. 11, edited by Frank E. Gaebelein, 341–418. Grand Rapids: Zondervan, 1978.

Ehrman, Bart D. *The New Testament: A Historical Introduction to the Early Christian Writings*. New York: Oxford, 1997.

Elwell, Walter A. *Encountering the New Testament*. Grand Rapids: Baker, 1997.

Epstein, I., ed. The *Babylonian Talmud* (Seder Nashim). 4 vols. London: Soncino, 1936/1938.

Eusebius. "Ecclesiastical History." In *The Nicene and Post-Nicene Fathers, Second Series Vol. 1–Eusebius: Church History, Life of Constantine the Great, Oration in Praise of Constantine*. Edited by P. Schaff. Oak Harbor, WA: Logos Research Systems, 1997.

Evans, Craig A., and Stanley E. Porter, eds. *Dictionary of New Testament Background*. Downers Grove, IL: Intervarsity, 2000.

Fee, Gordon D. *1 and 2 Timothy, Titus*. Peabody, MA: Hendrickson, 1995.

———. "Reflections on Church Order in The Pastoral Epistles, With Further Reflections on The Hermeneutics of Ad Hoc Documents." *Journal of the Evangelical Theological Society* 28 (1985) 142–52.

Fee, Gordon, D., and Douglas Stuart. *How to Read the Bible for All its Worth*. London: Scripture Union, 1982.

Freedman, David N., ed. *The Anchor Bible Dictionary*. Vol. 2. New York: Doubleday, 1992.

Friesen, Stephen J. "The Cult of the Roman Emperors in Ephesos—Temple Wardens, City Titles, and the Interpretation of the Revelation of John." In *Ephesos, Metropolis of Asia*, edited by Herman Koester, 229–50. Valley Forge: Harvard Theological Studies, 1995.

Bibliography

———. *Twice Neokoros Ephesus, Asia and the Cult of the Flavian Imperial Family*. Religions in the Graeco-Roman World 116. Leiden: E. J. Brill, n.d.

Gealy, Fred. "First and Second Epistles to Timothy and the Epistle to Titus" (exegesis only). In *The Interpreters Bible*, vol. 11. Nashville: Abingdon, 1955.

Gill, Malcolm. *Jesus as Mediator*. Oxford: Peter Lang, 2008

Glasscock, Ed. "The Biblical Concept of Elder." *Bibliotheca Sacra* 144 (1987) 67–79.

Goodspeed, E. J. "The Place of Ephesus in Early Christian Literature: New Chapters in New Testament Study." New York, 1937.

Gordon, Alan. "James: Diatribe, Paraenesis or Protreptic Discourse? The Hellenistic Subgenre of the Letter of James." Dr. Th. diss., Australian College of Theology.

Graves, Robert. *The Greek Myths*. Vol. 1. London: Folio Society, 1996.

Greenhalgh, Michael. *The Greek and Roman Cities of Western Turkey*. http://rubens.anu.edu.au/raider4/turkey/turkeybook/intro1.html.

Gregory of Nyssa. "Sermons on the Lord's Prayer 5." Quoted in Barclay, William. *The Lord's Prayer*. Westminster: John Knox, 1998.

Gritz, Sharon H. *Paul, Women Teachers, and the Mother Goddess at Ephesus*. Lanham: University Press of America, 1991.

Guthrie, Donald. *New Testament Introduction*. Downers Grove, IL: Intervarsity, 1990.

———. *The Pastoral Epistles*. Grand Rapids: Wm. B. Eerdmans, 1957.

Guy, H. A. *The Gospel of Mark*. Basingstoke: Macmillan Education, 1968.

Hansen, William, ed. "The Acts of Paul and Thecla." In *Anthology of Ancient Greek Popular Literature*, translated by R. McL. Wilson, 55–63. Bloomington: Indiana University Press, 1998.

Harland, Philip A. "Honours and Worship: Emperors, Imperial Cults and Associations at Ephesus (first to third centuries c.e.)." *Studies in Religion/Sciences Religieuses* 25 (1996) 319–34. http://www.philipharland.com/publications/Harland%201996%20Honours%20Ephesos.pdf.

Harris, Timothy J. "Why Did Paul Mention Eve's Deception? A Critique of P. W. Banett's Interpretation of 1 Timothy 2." *Evangelical Quarterly* 62 (1990) 335–52.

Hauck, Friedrich. "κόπος, κοπιάω." In *Theological Dictionary of the New Testament*, edited by G. Kittel, et al., 3.827–30. Grand Rapids: Eerdmans, 1964.

Hawthorne, Gerand F., and Ralph P. Martin, eds. *Dictionary of Paul and His Letters*. Downers Grove, IL: Intervarsity, 1993.

Hendriksen, William. *1&2 Thessalonians, 1&2 Timothy & Titus*. Edinburgh: Banner of Truth, 1983.

Herodotus. *The Histories*. Translated by Aubrey De Selincourt. Harmondsworth: Penguin, 1954.

Hesiod. "The Homeric Hymns." In *Works of Hesiod and the Homeric Hymns*. Translated by Darryl Hine. Chicago: Chicago University Press, 2005.

Bibliography

Hiebert, Edmond. *First Timothy.* Chicago: Moody, 1957.

———. "Titus." In *The Expositors Bible Commentary,* vol. 11, edited by Frank E. Gaebelein, 421–49. Grand Rapids: Zondervan, 1978.

Hippolytus. "Refutation of All Heresies." In *The Ante-Nicene Fathers.* Vol. 5, *Translations of the Writings of the Fathers Down to A.D. 325. Fathers of the Third Century: Hippolytus, Cyprian, Novatian, Appendix.* Edited by A. Roberts, et al. Oak Harbor, WA: Logos Research Systems, 1997:

Hoag, Gary G. *Wealth in Ancient Ephesus and the First Letter to Timothy. Fresh Insights from Ephesiaca by Xenophon of Ephesus.* Winona Lake: Eisenbrauns, 2015.

Howe, E. Margaret. "The Positive Case for the Ordination of Women." In *Perspectives in Evangelical Theology,* edited by K. Kantzer and S. Gundry, 276. Grand Rapids: Baker, 1979.

Hübner, Jamin. "Revisiting αὐθεντέω in 1 Timothy 2:12: What Do the Extant Data Really Show." *Journal for the Study of Paul and His Letters* 5.1 (2015) 42–70.

Hugenberger, Gordon F. "Women in Church Office: Hermeneutics or Exegesis? A Survey of Approaches to 1 Tim 2:8–15." *Journal of the Evangelical Theological Society* 35.3 (1992) 41–360.

Hughes, R. Kent. "Living Out God's Order in the Church." *The Master's Seminary Journal* 10 (1999) 102–12.

Huizenga, Annette B. *1–2 Timothy, Titus.* Collegeville, PA: Liturgical, 2016.

Ignatius. "Epistle to the Magnesians." In *The Ante-Nicene Fathers.* Vol. 1, *Translations of the Writings of the Fathers Down to A.D. 325. The Apostolic Fathers with Justin Martyr and Irenaeus.* Edited by A Roberts, et al. Oak Harbor, WA: Logos Research Systems, 1997.

———. "Epistle to the Smyrnaeans." In *The Ante-Nicene Fathers.* Vol. 1, *Translations of the Writings of the Fathers Down to A.D. 325. The Apostolic Fathers with Justin Martyr and Irenaeus.* Edited by a. Roberts, et al. Oak Harbor, WA: Logos Research Systems, 1997.

———. "Epistle to the Trallains." In *The Ante-Nicene Fathers.* Vol. 1, *Translations of the Writings of the Fathers Down to A.D. 325. The Apostolic Fathers with Justin Martyr and Irenaeus.* Edited by A. Roberts, et al. Oak Harbor, WA: Logos Research Systems, 1997.

Irenaeus. "Against Heresies." In *The Ante-Nicene Fathers.* Vol. 1, *Translations of the Writings of the Fathers Down to A.D. 325. The Apostolic Fathers with Justin Martyr and Irenaeus.* Edited by A Roberts, et al. Oak Harbor, WA: Logos Research Systems, 1997.

Isocrates. *Isocrates with an English Translation in Three Volumes.* Translated by George Norlin. Cambridge: Harvard University Press, 1980.

Johnson, Luke Timothy. *The First and Second Letters to Timothy.* New Haven: Yale University Press. 2001.

Josephus. "Antiquities." In *Josephus–Complete Works.* Translated by William Whiston. London: Pickering and Inglis, 1960.

Bibliography

Justin Martyr. "Dialogue with Trypho, a Jew." In *The Ante-Nicene Fathers*, vol. 1, edited by Alexander Roberts and James Donaldson, 194–270. Peabody, MA: Hendrickson, 1995.

Juvenal. "Satires." In *Juvenal and Persius*, edited and translated by Susanna Morten Braune. Loeb Classical Library 91. Cambridge: Harvard University Press, 2004.

Keener, Craig S. "Chapter 1." In *Two Views on Women in Ministry*, edited by James R. Beck and Craig L Bloomberg. Grand Rapids: Zondervan, 2001

———. *Paul, Women and Wives—Marriage and Women's Ministry in the Letters of Paul*. Peabody, MA: Hendrickson, 1992.

———. "Was Paul For or Against Women in Ministry?" *Enrichment Journal* (Spring 2001) 82–86. https://www.craigkeener.com/wp-content/uploads/2019/09/EJ_2001_02_Spring_Keener-1.pdf.

Kelly, J. N. D. *Commentary on the Pastoral Epistles*. Grand Rapids: Barker, 1981.

Kent, Homer A. *The Pastoral Epistles*. Chicago: Moody, 1958.

Knibbe, Dieter. "Via Sacra Ephesiaca." In *Ephesos, Metropolis of Asia*, edited by Herman Koester, 141–56. Valley Forge: Harvard Theological Studies, 1995.

Koester, Herman. "Ephesos in Early Christian Literature." In *Ephesos, Metropolis of Asia*, edited by Herman Koester, 119–56. Valley Forge: Harvard Theological Studies, 1995.

Köstenberger, Andreas J. "Saved Through Childbearing? A Fresh Look at 1 Timothy 2:15 Points to Protection from Satan's Deception." *Journal for Biblical Manhood and Womanhood* 2.4 (1997) 1, 3–6.

Kraft, Robert A., trans. "The Didache." In *The Apostolic Fathers*, vol. 3. Toronto: Thomas Nelson and Son, 1965.

Lee, Thomas D., and Hayne P. Griffin. *1, 2 Timothy, Titus*. Nashville: Broadman & Holman, 1992.

Lemcio, Eugene E. "Ephesus and the New Testament Canon," *John Rylands University Library of Manchester* 69 (1986–87) 210–34.

LiDonnici, Lynn R. "The Image of Artemis Ephesia in Greco-Roman Worship: A Reconstruction." *Harvard Theological Review* 85.4 (1992) 389–415.

Liefeld, Walter L. *1 & 2 Timothy, Titus*. Grand Rapids: Zondervan, 1999.

———. "A Plural Ministry View." *Women in Ministry, Four Views*, edited by Bonnidell Clouse and Robert G. Clouse, 127–53. Downers Grove, IL: IVP Academic, 1989.

Lock, Walter. *The Pastoral Epistles*. Edinburgh: T and T Clark, 1978.

MacRae, George W., trans. "Apocalypse of Adam." *Early Christian Writings*. http://www.earlychristianwritings.com/text/adam.html.

Mappes, David A. "The Discipline of a Sinning Elder." *Bibliotheca Sacra* 154 (1997) 334–34.

———. "The Heresy Paul Opposed in 1 Timothy." *Bibliotheca Sacra* 156 (1999) 452–59.

———. "The 'Laying on of Hands' of Elders." *Bibliotheca Sacra* 154 (1997) 457–97.

Bibliography

———. "Moral Virtues Associated with Eldership." *Bibliotheca Sacra* 160 (2003) 203–19.

———. "The New Testament Elder, Overseer, and Pastor." *Bibliotheca Sacra* 154 (1997) 163–75.

Mickelsen, Alvera. "An Egalitarian View: There Is Neither Male nor Female." In *Women in Ministry, Four Views*, edited by Bonnidell Clouse and Robert G. Clouse, 173–205. Downers Grove, IL: IVP Academic, 1989.

The Mishna. Translated by Jacob Neusner. New Haven: Yale University Press, 1988.

Moo, Douglas J. "1 Timothy 2:11–15: Meaning and Significance." *Trinity Journal* ns 1.1 (1980) 62–83.

———. "The Interpretation of 1 Timothy 2:11–15: A Rejoinder." *Trinity Journal* 2.2 (1981) 199–213.

Moore, Terri Darby. *If They Remain: An Analysis of Approaches to 1 Timothy 2:15*. https://bible.org/series/if-they-remain-analysis-approaches-1-timothy-215.

Mounce, William D. *Pastoral Epistles*. Nashville: Thomas Nelson, 2000.

Noyes, Morgan P. "First and Second Epistles to Timothy and the Epistle to Titus" (exposition only). In *The Interpreters Bible*, vol. 11. Nashville: Abingdon, 1955.

Oldfather, William A. "Introduction." In *Aeneas Tacticus, Asclepiodotus, Onasander*. Loeb Classical Library 156. Cambridge: Harvard University Press, 1923.

Onasander. *Aeneas Tacticus, Asclepiodotus, Onasander*. Loeb Classical Library 156. Cambridge: Harvard University Press, 1923.

Oster Richard E. "Ephesus." In *The Anchor Bible Dictionary* 2. Edited by David N. Freedman. New York: Doubleday, 1992.

Padgett, Alan. "Wealthy Women at Ephesus 1 Timothy 2:8–15 in Social Context." *Interpretation* 41 (1987) 19–31.

Pausanias. *Description of Greece*. 4 Vols. Translated by W. H. S. Jones and H. A. Ormerod. Cambridge: Harvard University Press, 1918.

Payne, Philip B. "Libertarian Women in Ephesus: A Response to Douglas J. Moo's Article, '1 Timothy 2:11–15: Meaning and Significance.'" *Trinity Journal* 2 (1981) 170–98.

———. *Man and Woman, One in Christ: An Exegetical and Theological Study of Paul's Letters*. Grand Rapids: Zondervan, 2009.

Pietersen, Lloyd K. *The Polemic of the Pastorals*. London: T&T Clark, 1994.

Plautus, T. Maccius. "Miles Gloriosus, or The Braggart Captain." In *The Comedies of Plautus*, translated by Henry Thomas Riley. London. G. Bell and Sons, 1912.

Pliny. *Letters*. Translated by William Melmoth and revised by W. M. L. Hutchinson. London: William Heinemann, 1931.

Pliny the Elder. "The Natural History." In *Pliny the Elder*, translated by John Bostock and H. T. Riley. London: Taylor and Francis, 1855.

Polycarp. "Epistle to the Philippians." In *The Ante-Nicene Fathers*. Vol. 1, *Translations of the Writings of the Fathers Down to A.D. 325. The Apostolic*

Bibliography

Fathers with Justin Martyr and Irenaeus. Edited by A. Roberts, et al. Oak Harbor, WA: Logos Research Systems, 1997.

Reicke, Bo. "προστῆναι." In *Theological Dictionary of the New Testament.* ed. G. Kittel, G. W. Bromiley and G. Friedrich, 6.700–703. Grand Rapids: Eerdmans, 1964.

Rengstorf, Karl Heinrich. "διδάσκω." In *Theological Dictionary of the New Testament,* edited by G. Kittel, G. W. Bromiley, 2.135–65. Grand Rapids: Eerdmans, 1964.

Safrai, S., and M. Stern, eds. *The Jewish People in the First Century Historical Geography, Political History, Social, Cultural and Religious Life and Institutions.* Vol. 1. Assen: Van Gorcum, 1974.

———. *The Jewish People in the First Century Historical Geography, Political History, Social, Cultural and Religious Life and Institutions.* Vol. 2. Assen: Van Gorcum, 1976.

Saucy, Robert L. "The Husband of One Wife." *Bibliotheca Sacra* 131 (1974) 230–42.

———. "Women's Prohibition to Teach Men: An Investigation into Its Meaning and Contemporary Application." *Journal of the Evangelical Theological Society* 37.1 (1994) 80–99.

Schreiner, Thomas R. "Chapter 3." In *Two Views on Women in Ministry,* edited by James R. Beck and Craig L Bloomberg. Grand Rapids: Zondervan, 2001.

———. "An Interpretation of 1 Timothy 2:9–15." In *Women in the Church: An Interpretation and Application of 1 Timothy 2:9–15,* edited by Andreas J. Kostenberger and Thomas R. Schreiner, 163–225. Wheaton, IL: Crossway, 2016.

Semmler, Michael P. *Introduction to the Summaries of the Teaching of the Ordination of Men Only and The Case for the Ordination of Women.* Lutheran Church of Australia, 2008.

Spencer, Aida Besancon. "Eve at Ephesus (Should Women Be Ordained as Pastors According to The First Letter to Timothy 2:11–15)." *Journal of the Evangelical Theological Society* 17.4 (1974) 220–30.

———. "Leadership of Women in Crete and Macedonia as a Model for the Church." *Priscilla Papers* 27.4 (2013) 5–12.

Stiefel, Jennifer H. "Women Deacons in 1 Timothy: A Linguistic and Literary Look at 'Women Likewise . . . ' (1 Tim 3.11)." *New Testament Studies* 41.3 (1995) 442–57.

Stock, Eugene. *Practical Truths from the Pastoral Epistles.* Grand Rapids: Kregel, 1983.

Strabo. *The Geography of Strabo,* vols. 1–7, translated by Horace L Jones. Loeb Classical Library 49, 50, 182, 196, 211, 223. Cambridge: Harvard University Press 1923–32.

Strelan, Rick. *Paul, Artemis, and the Jews.* Berlin: Walter de Gruyter, 1996.

Stubbersfield, Edgar. *Ephesus—Its History and Religious Setting.* Gatton: Rachel Stubbersfield, 2006.

Bibliography

———. *Introduction to the Pastoral Epistles*. Gatton: Rachel Stubbersfield, 2013.
Tacitus, Publius Cornelius. "The Annals." In *The Complete Works of Tacitus*, translated by Alfred John Church, et al. New York: Random House, 1942.
Tatius, Achilles. "The Adventures of Leucippe and Clitophon." In *Achilles Tatius*. Translated by S. Gaselee. Loeb Classical Library 45. London: William Heineman, 1917.
Tertullian. "Against Marcion." in *The Ante-Nicene Fathers*. Vol. 3, *Translations of the Writings of the Fathers Down to A.D. 325. Latin Christianity: Its Founder, Tertullian*. Edited by A. Roberts, et al. Oak Harbor, WA: Logos Research Systems, 1997.
———. "On Baptism." In *The Ante-Nicene Fathers*. Vol. 3, *Translations of the Writings of the Fathers Down to A.D. 325. Latin Christianity: Its Founder, Tertullian*. Edited by A. Roberts, et al. Oak Harbor, WA: Logos Research Systems, 1997.
Thomas, Christine M. "At Home in the City of Artemis—Religion in Ephesos in the Literary Imagination of the Roman Period." In *Ephesos, Metropolis of Asia*, edited by Herman Koester, 81–118. Valley Forge: Harvard Theological Studies, 1995.
Towner, P. H. "Gnosis and Realized Eschatology in Ephesus (of the Pastoral Epistles) and the Corinthian Enthusiasm." *Journal for the Study of the New Testament* 31 (1987) 95–124.
Trebilco, Paul R. *Jewish Communities in Asia Minor*. Cambridge: Cambridge University Press, 1991.
Trombley, Frank R. "Paganism in the Greek World at the End of Antiquity: The Case for Rural Anatolia and Greece." *Harvard Theological Review* 78 (1985) 327–52.
Vermes, Geza, trans. "The Community Rule (1QS)." In *The Complete Dead Sea Scrolls in English*, Rev. Ed., 97–117. Penguin: London, 2004.
Von Campenhausen, Hans. *Ecclesiastical Authority and Spiritual Power*. Translated by J. A. Baker. Stanford: Stanford University Press 1969.
Wallace, Daniel B., and Michael H. Burer. "Was Junia Really an Apostle? A Reexamination of Romans 16:7." *Journal for Biblical Manhood and Womanhood* 6.2 (2001) 4–11.
Walters, James C. "Egyptian Religions in Ephesos." In *Ephesos, Metropolis of Asia*, edited by Herman Koester, 281–310. Valley Forge: Harvard Theological Studies, 1995.
Waltke, Bruce K. "1 Timothy 2:8–15: Unique or Normative?" *Journal for Biblical Manhood and Womanhood* 1.4 (1996) 4–7.
White, L. Michael. "Urban Development and Social Change in Imperial Ephesus." In *Ephesos, Metropolis of Asia*, edited by Herman Koester, 27–80. Valley Forge: Harvard Theological Studies, 1995.
Wilson, Geoffrey B. *The Pastoral Epistles*. Edinburgh: Banner of Truth, 1982.
Wilson, Stephen G. *Luke and the Pastoral Epistles*. London: SPCK, 1979.
Wisse, Frederik, trans. "Apocryphon of John." *Early Christian Writings*. http://www.earlychristianwritings.com/text/apocryphonjohn.html.

Bibliography

Wolters, Al. "The Meaning of Αὐθεντεῖν." In *Women in the Church: An Interpretation and Application of 1 Timothy 2:9–15*, edited by Andreas J. Kostenberger and Thomas R. Schreiner, 65–115. 3rd edition. Wheaton, IL: Crossway, 2016.

Xenophon of Ephesus. "An Ephesian Tale." In *Anthology of Ancient Greek Popular Literature*, edited by William Hansen and translated by Moses Hadas, 3–49. Bloomington: Indiana University Press, 1998.

Yarbrough, Robert W. "Familiar Paths and a Fresh Matrix." In *Women in the Church: An Interpretation and Application of 1 Timothy 2:9–15*, edited by Andreas J. Kostenberger and Thomas R. Schreiner, 227–77. 3rd edition. Wheaton, IL: Crossway, 2016.

Young, Frances. *The Theology of the Pastoral Letters*. Cambridge: Cambridge University Press, 1994.

Zodhiates, S. *The Complete Word Study Dictionary*: New Testament (electronic ed.). AMG Publishers: Chattanooga, c. 1992 and 1993.

www.ingramcontent.com/pod-product-compliance
Lightning Source LLC
Chambersburg PA
CBHW050837160426
43192CB00011B/2063